DISCARDED

DISCARDED

THE
GOOD
BOOK
and
GOOD BUSINESS

How to Succeed the Christian Way

CRANE HILL
PUBLISHERS

The Good Book and Good Business
How to Succeed the Christian Way

Copyright © 2006 Gary W. Hutto
Book design by Miles G. Parsons

All rights reserved. With the exception of brief quotations in critical reviews or articles, no part of this work may be reproduced or transmitted in any form or by any means, electronic or mechanical, including photocopying, recording, or any information storage and retrieval system, without permission in writing from the publisher.

Scripture taken from the HOLY BIBLE: NEW INTERNATIONAL VERSION®. NIV®. Copyright © 1973, 1978, and 1984 by International Bible Society. Used by permission of The Zondervan Corporation.

The "NIV" and "New International Version" trademarks are registered in the United States Patent and Trademark Office by International Bible Society. All rights reserved.

This publication is designed to provide general information and practical guidelines for application of the Holy Bible to business. The author is not an attorney, and the book is not a legal reference. Neither the author nor publisher is rendering management, accounting, or legal advice, and will not be responsible for any loss or damage allegedly arising from any information or suggestion in this book.

Selected passages in Chapter 6 are based on text from the *Handbook of Mortgage Banking Financial Management*, Second Edition, Copyright 2005, authored by Gary W. Hutto and published by the Mortgage Bankers Association. Such portions are included herein with the express permission of the Mortgage Bankers Association, Washington, DC (http:www.mbaa.org). All rights reserved.

Library of Congress Cataloging-in-Publication Data

Hutto, Gary W., 1950-
   The good book and good business / by Gary W. Hutto.
   p. cm.
   ISBN-13: 978-1-57587-258-2
   1. Business--Religious aspects--Christianity. I. Title.
   HF5388.H88 2005
   261.8'5--dc22
      2006011646

THE
GOOD
BOOK

and

GOOD BUSINESS

How to Succeed the Christian Way

GARY W. HUTTO, CPA, AMP

CRANE HILL
PUBLISHERS

TABLE OF CONTENTS

PREFACE

First, to my clients, you are not in here; so if you think you are, you are not. As you know, I owe you a duty of confidentiality—a duty that I take quite seriously.

Second, family, friends, and church family, except for one mention of my Thursday morning prayer group and one mention of my pastor, Ron Sumners, you are not in here either. So do not bother looking for yourself. I would break the Golden Rule if I talked about any of you and you know I would not anyway—besides no one ever tells me anything interesting.

All kidding aside, writing this book was quite humbling. I feel like the Apostle Paul because I know as he did that I am the greatest of all sinners. I also know that whatever I try not to do, I continually do anyway. In other words, I sin even when I do not want to do so—which requires a lot of repenting and praying on my part. Therefore, I ask the readers of this book for some forbearance because many times I am preaching to myself. Because of writing this book, I understand how poorly I have applied the Good Book to good business and to a good life. However, I do not feel like a hypocrite in telling you about the truths of the Good Book because writing and researching the book has done me more good than it will ever probably do for you, although I hope it proves useful for you as well. What I am really trying to say is writing the book was almost like a recommitment to the Lord's principles. Regardless, I can still try to communicate to you what I have learned and experienced.

I have not used gender neutrality even though I am anti-racist and anti-sexist, if that is a word, but I think you catch the drift. I believe in equal rights for all people and the equal application of the laws to all because that is what the Bible teaches.

However, since I am growing old, I find it hard to change

my old writing habits. Accordingly, I use male pronouns throughout this book because it was just easier for me to write that way and some of the "person" words do not flow very well. Regardless, I would like my women friends and sisters in Christ to know that every time I use the masculine gender I thought of you in the way that Paul in Galatians suggested I feel. That is, without discrimination for anyone, knowing that we are all equal in Christ. Accordingly, I have not excluded you—please forgive me for writing the way my English teachers taught me to write. I am just glad I am not French because every noun in French is either male or female.

Last, before you start reading this book, I ask you to pray for me. I need better application of the teaching of Jesus in my own life and work. I will pray for you also.

ACKNOWLEDGMENTS

I would like to thank Crane Hill Publishers and my editor, Linda Beam, for giving me the opportunity to write this book.

Of course, my wife, Becky, kept me on track and constantly told me that, "I had a book to write." Her reminders were especially helpful during what has turned into one of the more hectic years of my life. Becky encouraged me and helped me with formatting of footnotes and the bibliography, which I always hate doing, so I very much appreciate her help in that area. Thanks Bec for the help and encouragement.

While my writing often made Maggie and Brady, my faithful Springer Spaniel writing companions, soporific, I appreciated their company and inspiration anyway.

I would also like to thank my understanding and loving Sunday School class at Meadow Brook Baptist Church in Birmingham, Alabama. Without their love and support, I do not know how I would have made it through the past several years. My Thursday morning prayer group has also kept me uplifted in their prayers and I thank you guys for that.

I also owe thanks to the editors who have published my other books and articles over the years. These great people have often brightened my day with a call or an e-mail—particularly, Rose Ann Dobbins, Neil Morse, Adina Holmes, John Florian, Ruth Fields, Janet Hewitt, Connie Lepore, and Michael Kling.

I would also like to thank my dad, my mother, and my father-in-law, Bryce Martin. My dad, a retired Unites States Air Force Senior Master Sergeant, taught me many of the management techniques that he learned through the school of hard knocks or what he liked to call on-the-job training. Since my dad is struggling with Alzheimer's, I do not know whether he will be able to read and understand this acknowledgment, but thanks, Dad, for teaching me some of your tried and true management techniques. My mom taught me about compassion, giving, non-discrimination, and striving to better one's self through learning. Mr. Martin, my deceased father-in-law (I never called him Bryce as long as he lived), taught me humility and the application of the Golden Rule—he always helped those who needed it and generally did it quietly, without the need for acclamation—thanks, Bryce, for being the humble, practicing Christian man and father you were.

Again, thanks to all of you,

Gary Hutto
May 24, 2006

Chapter 1

Principles of the Good Book

It is important to understand the relationship of the Old and New Testaments before we start our study of the Good Book and good business. This book will discuss the principles underlying both testaments as it illustrates the application of the Good Book to good business. Accordingly, the reader must understand this author's viewpoint regarding the relationship of the two testaments in order to understand why the author emphasizes the importance of certain biblical teachings and their application to good business.

The Consistency of the Old and New Testaments

In the study of the relationship of the two testaments, some view the Old and New Testament as two different views of God's will—as if God displayed his will to mankind one way to certain peoples and in another way to other peoples. However, other students of the Bible, including the author of this book, view the two testaments holistically as part and parcel of universal truth—that is, the Old Testament leads to the New Testament, but the truth underlying them both is the same. For as Jesus said, "I have not come to rid you of the law but to fulfill it." [Author's paraphrase—see Matthew 5:17.] In this context, the word fulfill does not mean to annul but rather to complete—or, you could say that Jesus came to complete the revelation of God's universal truth.

The Old Testament consists primarily of the law, history, poetry/wisdom, and the prophets. The first five books of the Bible, often called the Torah or the Pentateuch (which in Latin just means five books), contain the Laws (or collectively, the Law) sent by God, via Moses, to God's people, the Hebrews. As you will recall, the Hebrews are Abraham's descendants through his legitimate son, Isaac, who was miraculously conceived when his mother, Sarah, was too old to bear children. Abraham had another son, Ishmael, by his wife's handmaiden, Hagar, through whom the Moslems and Arabs trace their relationship to Abraham.

The Law consists of more than just the Ten Commandments given directly to Moses by God for use by his people, the Hebrews. It also includes a number of ethical, religious, societal, and business precepts, rules, regulations, and interpretations as well. The Jews retained much of this non-Torah law (that is, the five books of the law) in an oral tradition from the time of Moses to the time of Judah the Patriarch in the second century AD, when the Jews finally wrote the oral tradition down. The Jews refer to this oral tradition as the Mishnah, which means to repeat. That is how the Jews managed to preserve the oral tradition— memorization through repeated spoken readings of the Mishnah from the teacher to the student.

Almost the whole Old Testament deals tangentially with the Law. For example, the history books describing the reigns of the judges and the kings once the Hebrews entered the Promised Land all deal with the law. Similarly, the prophets who spoke to God's people and the Hebrew kings during the Old Testament's history all addressed the law—either when addressing the people or their leaders. Specifically, Old Testament history and the related prophesies (with limited exceptions) primarily concentrate on compliance or noncompliance with the Law by the Israelites (generally, the latter—that is, their noncompliance).

Sunday school classes often complain about studying the Old Testament since it seems to deal primarily with doom, gloom, destruction, sin, and failure. However, one does not have to study the Old Testament very long before one finds a people not that psychologically or behaviorally different from modern mankind. Twenty-first century man still wars, kills, lies, extorts, and cheats. We also manage to create our own share of doom, gloom, destruction, sin, and failure.

Therefore, what we find when we study the Old Testament is that people have not changed, although their technologies for living may have (except in the poorest countries where things are not all that different than they were at the end of the Old Testament era). Although man may have changed outwardly, he is still the same old man on the inside. The sins we commit today are nothing new under the sun—the preacher in Ecclesiastes said so, and it's still true today.

The prophets generally warn the Israelites (with the exception of Jonah, who warned the Ninevites of Assyria) of their failure to comply with God's word and the consequences for not doing so. Sometimes the kings lead the Israelites to comply with the prophetic declarations, sometimes they did not, and sometimes they even defied the prophet (for instance, Ahab and his wife Jezebel defied the prophet Elijah—see 1 Kings chapters 16 through 22). Those that did not repent and change suffered the consequences of their actions (which are well documented in 1 and 2 Kings and 1 and 2 Chronicles).

However, ultimately God became so disgusted with the Israelite's apostasy that He allowed the Babylonians to conquer the Israelites, which resulted in exile of the Jewish leadership to Babylon (the Babylon Captivity). The sins that God could not tolerate and the sins that ultimately resulted in the Babylonian Captivity (or exile) included man putting God below the first position where He commanded them to hold Him and man's inhumanity to man—sound familiar?

After a scriptural hiatus of approximately five hundred years (between the writing of the last books of the Old Testament to the first writing of the New Testament), the New Testament came into being. The New Testament (which simply means the new covenant or contract) describes:

a) the activities, life, and work of Jesus Christ to fulfill the law,

b) the activities and testimony of the apostles in spreading the gospel (that is, the good news) to the known world, and

c) the theology of the new Christian Church (primarily contained in the writings of Paul).

Although the character and plot of the two testaments differ, the spiritual truth (or theme) underlying them is the same. It must be so; otherwise, God would prove capricious and inconsistent. That underlying and spiritual truth consists of God's love for whimsical, inconsistent, stubborn, and sinning mankind, which He first elucidated in the Old Testament and which he just continued in the New Testament. However, there is one major difference—in the New Testament, God displayed his love for mankind by sending his only Son to die a horrible death on a Roman cross so that we all might have life through his sacrificial death—a life that is available eternally for those that believe.

PILLARS OF THE BELIEVER'S WALK WITH GOD

Since God, the Bible (bible or biblos is simply the Greek word for book), and its truth are consistent and unchanging, the four pillars of a believer's walk are consistent and unchanging also. That is, what applied to the Old Testament believer's walk with God applies to the New Testament believer's walk with God. The four foundational pillars supporting the believer's walk upon God's walkway consist of:

1. the believer's love of God,
2. the believer's love of man,
3. the believer's faith in God, and
4. the believer's God-given wisdom.

LOVE OF GOD AND MAN

The believer's love of God is the first and greatest commandment. It is listed first in the Ten Commandments, requiring a believer to put Him first before everything else ("I am the Lord your God, who brought you out of Egypt, out of the land of slavery. You shall have no other gods before me."[1]). Further, Jesus named the love of God as the first of the two greatest commandments—that is, "Love the Lord your God with all your heart and with all your soul and with all your mind."[2] Interestingly, the command to love the Lord, quoted by Jesus in Matthew 22, comes from Deuteronomy 6, where the command to love the Lord is included in a prayer that begins with, "Hear O Israel, the Lord Our God, the Lord is one."[3] Obviously, when Jesus asserts that loving God is the greatest commandment, Jesus is one with God.[4] This oneness supports what we said previously; that is, the Old Testament leads to the New and the two are one. Further, there is no better evidence of this congruency and wholeness than when a) Jesus quotes directly from the Old Testament, and b) places God's first command in the same hierarchal order of obedience.

Jesus said the second greatest commandment is like the first. That is, as Moses wrote in Leviticus, we are to love man, specifically your neighbor. Of course, Moses was inspired and directed by God to tell us to love each other as we would ourselves. Specifically, in Leviticus 19:18, Moses instructed the Hebrews to "...not seek revenge or bear a grudge against one of your people, but love your neighbor as yourself. I am the Lord."[5]

Again, Jesus reemphasized the importance of loving your neighbor by stating that it was one of the two greatest commandments (see Matthew 22:37-40) and by quoting Leviticus 19:18 at Matthew 22:38. But, more importantly, as suggested previously, we again find the New Testament repeating the Old and with the same emphasis.

Love of your neighbor, which will be discussed more fully later, permeates the New Testament, including the famous passages contained in 1 Corinthians 13:

> When I was a child, I talked like a child, I thought like a child, I reasoned like a child. When I became a man, I put childish ways behind me. Now we see but a poor reflection as in a mirror; then we shall see face to face. Now I know in part; then I shall know fully, even as I am fully known. And now these three remain: faith, hope and love. But the greatest of these is *love*.[6] [Verse numbers omitted and emphasis added.]

John emphasizes the love of your neighbor in his first epistle, which includes these famous verses:

> This is the message you heard from the beginning: We should love one another. Do not be like Cain, who belonged to the evil one and murdered his brother. And why did he murder him? Because his own actions were evil and his brother's were righteous. Do not be surprised, my brothers, if the world hates you. *We know that we have passed from death to life, because we love our brothers. Anyone who does not love remains in death.* Anyone who hates his brother is a murderer, and you know that no murderer has eternal life in him. This is how we know what love is: Jesus Christ laid down his life for us. And we ought to lay down our lives for our brothers."[7] [Verse omitted and emphasis added.]

The reader should not find it surprising that the two of the four pillars of the believer's walk with God concern love—that is, love of God and love of humanity. After all, 1 John 4:16 states that "God is love."[8]

FAITH AND WISDOM

Faith is what it takes to accept God. As the New Testament book of Hebrews suggests, faith lies in the belief of things that are unseen ("…faith is being sure of what we hope for and certain of what we do not see…"[9]). A belief in God is obviously a belief in the unseen—with the limited exceptions of some Old Testament individuals, no one has ever seen God directly.

Faith is what it takes for one of us to accept God's grace (his merciful and unmerited favor), and faith is the key that God uses to open your soul so that the Holy Spirit may enter (as Jesus promised the Apostles that the Holy Spirit would do). Further, faith leads you to study God's commandments and instructions so that you, with the guidance of the Holy Spirit, will find the path of righteousness and remain on that path.

As mentioned above, faith leads one to study God's word, which leads a believer, with the assistance of the Holy Spirit, to wisdom. Bible study and the indwelling Holy Spirit will lead the believer not only to acquire wisdom, but also to practice God's teachings in his life, for as John says:

> The man who says, "I know him," [that is, Jesus] but does not do what he commands is a liar, and the truth is not in him. But if anyone obeys his word, God's love is truly made complete in him. This is how we know we are in him: Whoever claims to live in him *must walk as Jesus did.*[10] [Emphasis added.]

Some other sources of such wisdom, besides studying God's word, involve listening to Him, conversing with Him, confessing and admitting your failures to Him, asking for His guidance, attending Bible study, and listening to the preached word. In the author's opinion, the most important of these involves silently and openly communicating with God as you study His word and *listening* with your heart for His small, still, and soft voice of instruction so that we may, like Samuel, say, "Speak for your servant is listening."[11]

The remainder of this book will deal with the four pillars, or principles, in more detail and how the Good Book specifically applies to good business. May the Lord guide you to better management using the Good Book as your guide to good business—hopefully, you will be listening.

FOOTNOTES

[1] *The Holy Bible: New International Version*, (Grand Rapids, MI: Zondervan, 1996), Exod. 20:2-3.

[2] Matt. 22:37 NIV.

[3] Deut. 6:4 NIV.

[4] Obviously, under the doctrine of the trinity Jesus is one with God but as a different manifestation of Him. For example, see John Chapter 1 where it says: "In the beginning was the Word, and the Word was with God, and the Word was God. He was with God in the beginning. Through him all things were made; without him nothing was made that has been made. In him was life, and that life was the light of men." John 1:1-4 NIV.

[5] Lev. 19:18 NIV.

[6] 1 Cor. 13:11-13 NIV.

[7] 1 John 3:11-16 NIV.

[8] 1 John 4:16 NIV.

[9] Heb. 11:1 NIV.

[10] 1 John 2:4-6 NIV.

[11] 1 Sam 3:10 NIV.

CHAPTER 2

CHARACTERISTICS OF LEADERSHIP

James Collins, in *Good to Great, Why Some Companies Make the Leap and Others Don't*, points out that the primary characteristic of success for those companies that leap from good to great is leadership. Accordingly, since leadership is such an important part of business success, leadership will be discussed as the first part of the Good Book's application to good business, including specifically those leadership characteristics displayed in the Bible.

HUMILITY AND STRONG WILL

Contrary to what many would have intuitively expected, the best leaders were humble according to Collins, which is not very surprising to a student of scripture. In today's materialistic and individualistic culture, we have become accustomed to celebrity CEOs such as Jack Welch, formerly of GE, Martha Stewart, Leona Helmsley, or Lee Iacocca, formerly of Chrysler, whom we instantly recognize as successful, and who tend to egotistically celebrate his or her own celebrity.

However, Collins says that the CEOs of the great companies eschew celebrity. Society does not recognize those people or their successes because they stay in the background. Even if we sat next to them on an airplane, we would certainly not think that they ran a large company. For example, Collins mentions Darwin Smith, David Maxwell, Colman Mockler, Carl Reichardt, and Alan Wurtzel as examples of the humble CEO—not exactly CEOs touted in *Fortune*, *Business Week*, *Time*, *The Economist*, or *The Wall Street Journal*, and certainly not the names of CEOs that most of you would recognize (unless you read Collins' book). However, to provide some understanding of these men and their success, here is a list of companies they ran as CEOs:

- Smith was CEO of Kimberly-Clark
- Maxwell was CEO of Fannie Mae
- Mockler was CEO of Gillette
- Reichardt was CEO of Wells Fargo
- Wurtzel was CEO of Circuit City

Some believe that humility demonstrates weakness. These people believe that humility is a surefire way of not being noticed, promoted, or hired. In our individualistic culture, these egotistic types operate their own press agencies, issue their own press releases, and view not touting your own horn as a weakness or, perhaps, stupidity. We all know people who are always ready to take the credit but, in the alternative, when something bad happens, are always ready to place the blame on outside circumstances, or other people. This latter group of people obviously lacks humility.

In contrast, a humble person is comfortable with what he is, knows his strengths and weaknesses, does not run a press agency for himself, and does not have to be on the dais at every opportunity. Such people, according to Collins, give the credit to those in the company that actually create a success (that is, as Collins says, they look outward when success occurs), and solely take the blame when something bad occurs (that is, as Collins says, they look in the mirror).

Humility is a leadership characteristic found in Biblical leaders—that is why students of the Bible would not be surprised with the results of Collins' survey. Moses in the Old Testament is such an example.

When God called Moses, he was living as a Midianite shepherd. Although Moses was once Egyptian royalty, he had to leave Egypt because he killed an Egyptian who was beating a helpless Hebrew slave. After escaping Egypt, Moses settled in Midian and was now on the bottom of the social order—which in itself would prove a humbling experience to any man.

Nevertheless, God, from a burning bush, called Moses to lead the Hebrews from captivity in Egypt. Of course, in his current circumstances, Moses suggested that he was unworthy of God's call—"Who am I, that I should go to Pharaoh and bring the Israelites from Egypt?"[1] That was not an answer you would have expected from former royalty, but an answer you would expect from a man humbled by life's circumstances.

God assured Moses and told him that He would be with him. This is something every humble Christian called to service should remember. In God's service and in doing His will, the believer will always find comfort and support.

We also know that Moses proved to be a strong leader and one who, through love, interceded many times with God on the behalf of His obstinate, disrespectful, and disobeying people—the Israelites. He was strong because God had changed him—through his experience at Mount Sinai with the burning bush, his many altercations with Pharaoh, and the receipt of the Law from the hand of God.

The Bible also illustrates great leadership and political adroitness by telling the story of a humble Jew named Nehemiah, whose great service to Jerusalem was the rebuilding of its walls during the reign of the Persian King Artaxerxes.

Nehemiah was a trusted official of the Persian court and served Artaxerxes as his cupbearer. He asked Artaxerxes for permission to return to Jerusalem to help with its recovery after the Babylon Captivity. Because Nehemiah was such a strong and trusted leader, Artaxerxes appointed him to serve in the capacity of governor of Judah but only for a short while because he did not want to lose his services in Persia.

Nevertheless, Nehemiah's term of office as governor of Judah lasted twelve years (445 BC to 433 BC). During that time, he not only skillfully countered the opposition to the rebuilding of Jerusalem's walls, but also effectively administered the reconstruction of those walls (which only took fifty-two days) and the reinstallation of Jerusalem's city gates (which took a little longer). Nehemiah rallied the people to rebuild the walls when they doubted their ability to do so and organized protection of the reconstruction when those who did not desire its completion—the Arabs and Samaritans—threatened attack.

Nehemiah displayed humility as a leader by requesting permission from Artaxerxes to go to Jerusalem. He could have easily stayed in Persia and served Artaxerxes in a luxurious palace and in a place of honor as a court official. Rather, he left the comforts of the Persian king's palace and lived in Jerusalem, where an extensive process of reconstruction was taking place. Nehemiah did not live in luxury in Jerusalem, but shared his provisions with 150 people every day. Further, he did not seek his own enrichment and did not burden the people with unnecessary taxes (see Nehemiah 5:14-19).

In addition, Nehemiah displayed the will to get things done as he demonstrated by staving off the opposition to the rebuilding of Jerusalem's walls and by getting the walls built. This will, as Collins suggests, is a characteristic of a strong leader, whether in business or otherwise.

As Collins says a strong and humble leader would do,

Nehemiah 1) "create[d] superb results"[2] and 2) "[set] the standard of building an enduring [institution]."[3] Nehemiah satisfied Collins' first standard of a strong and humble leader by superbly repairing the walls in fifty-two days. Nehemiah met Collins' second standard through reemphasis of the Law, reinstitution of the Sabbath, and by his own example. In Nehemiah's reemphasis of the Law, he worked with Ezra to create a great religious revival among all the Jews—both those Jews returning to Palestine from Persia and those Jews who had remained in Palestine during the Babylon captivity.

Jesus himself placed a great emphasis on humility. For example, He blessed the humble in the Beatitudes (meaning blessings) contained in His Sermon on the Mount. In that sermon, He said that the humble would inherit the earth (see Matthew 5:5). Although the word for humble is often translated in English as the word meek (which has its own connotations of weakness), the root of the English word is the Greek word praus and its derivative praotes, according to William Barclay author of The Daily Study Bible Series. Both words suggest a humility that exhibits itself in recognition that God is supreme. The words also suggest that we, no matter how strong we may be on this earth, are nothing before Him. As the Psalmist said, "What is man that you are mindful of him?"[4]

God's humility also demonstrates a desire for more learning and a desire to obtain wisdom. Again, the humble man knows he does not know everything and is not so arrogant that he hides his ignorance.

God's humility also involves a love for man. A humble man realizes that God loves him and, since God loves him, the humble man realizes that he should do likewise.

Barclay says that we cannot accurately translate the words praus and praotes into English because of the many Greek meanings associated with the two words. However, he does translate the beatitude about the meek (or the humble if you will) as follows:

> O the bliss of the man who always angry at
> the right time and never angry at the wrong
> time, who has every instinct, and impulse,
> and passion under control because he himself
> is God-Controlled, who has the humility to
> realize his own ignorance and his own
> weakness, for such a man is a king among
> men!"[5]

I am sure Collins would agree with Barclay's description of a humble man since the characteristics Collins attributes to a strong and humble leader (what Collins calls a Level 5 leader, which is his highest and best leadership category) include the characteristics that Barclay uses to describe a humble man. Collins views a Level 5 leader as a paradox because he finds humility and strength coexisting in one man. That is, the Level 5 leader possesses humility and a strong "professional will."[6]

Collins found that some of the so-called Level 5 leaders had had some life changing experience that proved a catalyst for converting otherwise ordinary men to those who were both humble and strong. Not surprisingly, at least to a Christian, Collins suggests a linkage between religion and some of the Level 5 CEOs. For example, Collins says, "A strong religious belief or conversion *might* also nurture development of Level 5 traits."[7] [Emphasis added.]

The author of this book has a great deal of respect for Dr. Collins. The author has also gained much management insight from his books, *Built to Last* and *Good to Great*. However, the author has to disagree with the use of the word *might* by Dr. Collins when he uses the word in describing the development of Level 5 traits. These traits mirror those of many great leaders in the Bible and even of Jesus himself. Remember that Jesus was quite humble but was also quite strong when the circumstances required it (e.g., among other things, his many confrontations with the scribes and Pharisees and the righteous anger He displayed in the Temple against the moneychangers and the sellers of sacrificial animals). In contrast to Collins, "...I am not ashamed, because I know whom I have believed, and am convinced that he is able to guard what I have entrusted to him for that day."[8] In other words, the author knows that He, Jesus, makes the difference.

Although the author is sure that Collins, Peters, Reichheld, Porras, Drucker, and other management theorists and writers never expected an evangelical Christian to use their books as examples of scriptural principles, it is indeed interesting how God uses man's work for His glory. This book will discuss some of their theories and will juxtapose them in relation to the Good Book's principles as we further investigate the Good Book and good business.

DELEGATION

Many people try to do too much—for example, the micromanager. He is by definition a Theory X manager[9] because he does not treat employees as adults and constantly monitors them.

Another poor manager is the manager that will not delegate. That does not necessarily mean that the manager is a Theory X manager because the fault may simply be that the manager does not know how to delegate or, sometimes, in the alternative, he may just enjoy doing what he does so much that he does not want to delegate the work to others (to his detriment, the author has suffered from liking to do things rather than getting all tasks performed).

Often poor managers are excellent performers at the level

just below manager and really do not want to manage or know how to manage. For example, companies often promote their best salesman to a sales manager position. Often this promotion proves a mistake because the salesman likes to sell, likes the relative freedom of selling, and likes going out to visit different people every day. For this person, the company does him a disservice by promoting him to sales manager because it creates a situation where the manager now feels hemmed in or caged.

In addition, he is not doing what he is good at. Further, the management job does not fulfill his need to be a winner or his need for recognition—in fact, the promotion will probably result in negative reinforcement rather than the positive reinforcement he received when selling.

Moses was one of those leaders who originally tried to do too much. For example, Moses took it upon himself to judge all the affairs of a wandering tribe consisting of over 1.5 million people.[10]

When Jethro (Moses' father-in-law) saw Moses judging all the people, he asked him why he was doing so. Of course, Jethro was wise and was a leader of his own people as a priest of Midian. (See Exodus 18:13-27).

Jethro told Moses that the load was too heavy for one man to carry and that Moses would wear himself out trying to handle such a responsibility (burn-out is a classic symptom often displayed by those who do not delegate duties). Accordingly, Jethro told Moses to select men with integrity, judgment, and ability to make decisions at the appropriate levels. If need be, the more complicated cases would work their way up to Moses through the layers of leadership, much like cases work their way up through the American judicial system.

In other words, in this structure, Moses was to judge the most important cases. In addition, and this is a very important point, Jethro told Moses that he needed to teach the people.

Management books such as Peters' *In Search of Excellence* tell us that relatively flat organizational structures are the best because they operate with less bureaucratic drag and communication difficulties. Of course, bureaucracy tends to create its own work to serve the needs of the bureaucracy—primarily to justify its existence. Such busy work tends to create inefficiency and inharmonious interpersonal relations, since bureaucracy often creates dissension because of its desire to control or restrict the activities of others in the organization.

Moses' organization chart was relatively flat considering the number of people that comprised the Exodus—four layers of management excluding Moses. Further, those people selected by Moses were hands-on, what we would call line supervisors, and directly involved with the people. This was good for the people because they were cared for and their needs meet—application of the Golden Rule, which we will talk about later.

The Lord also provided Moses a means to delegate religious duties and its bureaucracy. The Lord did so by creating religious specialists outside the operational line authority Moses had created.

The Lord instructed Moses to designate the Levites (the tribe of Levi) to perform various religious functions. In addition, the Lord had Moses make Aaron the first high priest and then made being a priest a hereditary right. In other words, the priests would only come from Aaron's descendants.

Also, notice that Moses did not make the mistake of choosing the wrong type of leaders. He selected the right type of people for the job. To repeat, he selected those with integrity, judgment, and ability to make decisions at the appropriate levels.

Collins noted in *Good to Great* that choosing the *right* people was one of the important characteristics of a great company. Collins even noted that the emphasis on people in

Built to Last was wrong—rather, he emphasized that a company needs to hire the right people. Of course, Jethro, a leader in Midianite management theory, already knew that and applied it during the time of Moses.

THE TONE AT THE TOP

Moses, in wisely listening and applying Jethro's teachings, found that he now had more time to teach. In fact, Jethro, as mentioned before, charged him with teaching the people. Accordingly, Moses was in charge of teaching the people, not only by instructing them as to the law and its various requirements, but also by creating a moral atmosphere, reinforcing core values, and setting the tone at the top.

Every ethical and effectively managed company today has its tone emanating from top (a point made by Collins and his partner Porras in *Built to Last*, and by Collins in *Good to Great*). Further, the Public Company Accounting Oversight Board (PCAOB), the entity responsible for setting the auditing standards of public companies that was created as the result of the accounting scandals of the early twenty-first century, also emphasizes a tone at the top when a company establishes its internal controls and codes of ethics. Such a tone reflects the integrity, the ethics, and the core ideology of the company. Moses set this tone at the top by teaching the people the laws God had given him and by obeying those laws.

The lesson for the management of a business comes from Moses' example. That is, the tone at the top must emanate from the top—the CEO cannot delegate this responsibility. In other words, if you try to set the tone at the top by delegating that duty to an underling or an underlying body, it will never work. Upper management involvement must create the culture and the example. It is necessary for upper management to set the tone and to establish the values to ensure that the company moves in the desired direction.

In addition, management must demonstrate the tone at the top by walking the walk (something that Moses generally did except, for example, at Meribah Kadesh when, in anger, he took his staff and struck the rock from which water was flowing). Remember that Moses received the tablets containing the Ten Commandments directly from God, which demonstrates that God believed him to be holy and willing to obey. Similarly, God directly spoke to Moses when he selected Moses to lead the people (not through a prophet but "one-on-one"). In his holiness and in his speaking to God, Moses demonstrated that he indeed was walking the walk or otherwise God would not have used him.

The importance of emphasizing holiness is this: a holy person is one that separates himself for God. In other words, a holy person separates himself from the world's values and commits himself to God's values. The separate one may fail as Paul alluded to in Romans, "For what I want to do I do not do, but what I hate I do."[11] Nevertheless, his goal is to be righteous as God is righteous. Of course, righteousness is a value that the world generally does not value. Rather, the world often values covetousness, selfishness, cruelty, anger, materialism, foolishness, and evil.

In contrast to Moses, the Israelites often *failed* to walk the walk. Moses continually chastised them when they failed and when they sinned. The Hebrews in the journey from Egypt to Palestine repeatedly sinned and only evaded complete destruction through Moses' intercession with God. As you will remember (at least from the movie *The Ten Commandments*), the Israelites constructed a golden calf to worship, complained about the food (and about everything else also), and failed to follow the Lord by faith into Palestine.

Moses saved them from destruction through prayer but could not prevent their ostracism from the Holy Land because they followed man's advice rather than God's direction. The first generation of the people of the Exodus were exiled to the wilderness because they listened to ten of the twelve spies sent to Palestine. These men counseled the Israelites not to enter the land because of the number of people there, the size of the men, and their walled cities. For their failure to go into the Holy Land, based on the erroneous advice of the ten spies, an entire generation of Israelites (excluding Caleb and Joshua, the only two spies who advised the Hebrews to follow God's will) died before the next generation was allowed into the Promised Land.

You could say that Moses set the tone at the top by walking the walk and talking the talk but he had a lot of teaching to do. Regardless, that teaching finally did take hold (as witnessed by the survival of Judaism into the twenty-first century and the reincarnation of the state of Israel). Part of the reason is because of the walks of Moses, Joshua, Ezra, Ruth, Esther, Josiah, David, Rahab, Abraham, Nehemiah, Daniel, etc. The Old Testament documents all of their walks, and God's love of a very, at times, unlovable people.

Moses left the words in the books of the Law as a demonstration of what disobedience to God can create and as a means to teach the Jews what was right and wrong. Moses also showed us in the books of the Law what type of people we should not be. Finally, Moses demonstrated what Senge says about leaders, "Ultimately, people follow people who believe in something and have the abilities to achieve results in the service of those beliefs."[12]

TEACHING

An effective leader also knows how to teach. Notice that Jethro, as an instrument of God, advised Moses to instruct the people. Here it meant that the people would learn the Law—a Law that had not previously existed.

The Law taught more than religious observance; it also taught the ethics of everyday life and the ethics of business dealings, which the scribes and priests later expanded through an oral interpretation and then a written interpretation of that Law (but not until the second century AD). Similarly, top management of a company should teach the ethics of the company, determine its core values, and adopt the company's primary purpose. And, of course, top management should teach by leading as Moses, Joshua, and other religious leaders did.

Many entrepreneurs, such as the founder of Sony and the founders of Hewlett-Packard, were particularly adept at setting the tone at the top and teaching. However, as companies move from the entrepreneurial stage to the management phase, management often loses that entrepreneurial talent and ability. As supposition, that may be what happened when the kings started ruling Israel.

Or, in the alternative, the professional managers who take over running a company may overlook the need for this talent and ability. Besides, professional management may not really understand what the company does. Some act as if the company is just a vehicle for mergers or acquisitions, while others may think that all they have to do is market a company's products effectively. However, engineers such as the founders of Sony (Akio Morita) and Hewlett-Packard (Dave Packard and Bill Hewlett) understood the need to get out on the shop floor and demonstrate an interest in the people and the product.

In a recent television interview, Michael Dell, the founder

of Dell Computer, said that he often goes to the telephone center, where sales employees take orders, to feel the pulse of the company. He often takes a phone position himself and takes orders to stay in touch with the feelings of his customers. Perhaps other professional managers should do the same thing—maybe they would learn something.

Jesus also understood the need for training. Many of his parables were of direct benefit to his disciples and those who later became apostles. He would often take his disciples aside and explain his parables in more depth to broaden their understanding. For example, the apostle Mark emphasized Jesus' constant attention to the training of the disciples:

> With many similar parables Jesus spoke the word to them [the crowds], as much as they understand. He did not say anything to them without using a parable. But when he was alone with his own disciples, he explained everything.[13]

The disciples observed Jesus' humility, His effective teaching techniques, His love for people, and His ability to teach complicated subjects using stories. Obviously, from such close observation they learned what they would need to spread the gospel.

As you will remember, Jesus sent out seventy-two of His disciples into Palestine ahead of Him as witnesses for Him. His training prepared them to perform this witnessing work and this on-the-job training helped them even further with practical application of His teaching.

The training of the twelve apostles (excluding Judas but including Paul) was obviously excellent. Look at what they accomplished—those disciples evangelized much of the known world of that day (Thomas went as far as India, according to some commentators). Moreover, because of what they had learned, the apostles were then able to teach what Jesus had taught them.

The lesson for today's management is that just as Jesus taught the core values and ideology of the kingdom of heaven, company managers should demonstrate the core values and ideology of their companies. This means getting out of the executive suite (and perhaps destroying it in the process) and meeting and teaching those people who actually make the company run.

Although a company's CEO cannot reach or teach every employee of the company, it is, nevertheless, surprising how effective a CEO meeting the people in the plants, offices, and divisions is to a company's effectiveness. Even those employees whom the CEO does not meet knows he is there and that he cares enough to risk getting his pants dirty and his shoes scuffed to meet those who run the company at its most basic level.

When people believe they are valued, it is amazing what a difference they make to the company. Two of man's most important goals (after satisfying his basic survival needs) are a) being recognized, and b) being part of a winner. The CEO can do the former by making sure he gets out to his people (and not just the executives, managers, or foremen but the people on the line and the clerks in the office). The CEO should have his executives, managers, and foremen do likewise.

Obviously, the CEO and top management's ability to teach and learn are limited. However, the CEO and top management can, as suggested by Peter Senge in *The Fifth Discipline, The Art and Practice of the Learning Organization*, create a learning organization. This will only succeed if the leader of the company commits himself fully to teaching his people by creating such an organization.

BIBLICAL EXAMPLE OF A LEARNING ORGANIZATION

Interestingly, after the Babylon captivity, the Israelites needed to create a learning organization. While in Babylon, the people remaining in Palestine had lost their roots and a complete understanding of their religion since the Babylonians had taken the religious specialists (the priests and the Levites) away in the Babylon captivity. However, the Persian Kings, starting with Cyrus the Great and running through Artaxerxes, allowed the Jewish people to return. Zerubbabel, one returnee, rebuilt the temple and later Nehemiah rebuilt the walls of Jerusalem.

Ezra was a priest who returned thirteen years before Nehemiah. The book of Ezra indicates that Ezra was a man well qualified to create a learning institution (or, using Senge's terminology, a "learning organization") for the people of Israel. The Bible indicates that Ezra had these qualifications:

- He was a teacher well versed in the Law of Moses, which the Lord of God had given.[14]
- [The]…hand of the Lord his God was on him.[15]
- [He] had devoted himself to the study and observance of the Law of the Lord, and to teaching its decrees and laws in Israel.[16]

Ezra, using his knowledge of God, God's laws, and his wisdom, created a revival within the city of Jerusalem. This revival first consisted of reading the books of the law to the people and then reinstituting a) the feast of the tabernacles (or tents), b) the Temple procedures, and c) the laws against intermarriage.[17] Nehemiah, who was governor at the time, restored the laws regarding the Sabbath and upon his return from Persia, enforced the covenants the people had made during the revival but had then "neglected."[18]

All these efforts combined to bring a spiritual reawakening in Israel and the Jews, which created a foundation for a fluid but enduring set of laws, traditions, and regulations covering every facet of a Jewish person's life—including ethics, religion, social interaction, and business. This endurance allowed Judaism to survive the Diaspora of the Assyrian, Babylonians, and Romans and made it one of the world's oldest continuously practiced religions (probably only exceeded by Hinduism).

Until this time, expansions and interpretations of the law had relied on an oral tradition for their continued existence. The revival started by Ezra encouraged scribes, Levites, and priests to create a religion of study and meditation.

However, as important as the revival was to the reestablishment of Judaism among the people, Ezra's creation of the Great Assembly is probably more important since it, and other institutions, were responsible for ensuring the survival of the oral tradition until Judah the Patriarch codified those traditions into the book known as the Mishnah in the second century AD. The Great Assembly was charged with preserving the oral tradition and interpreting the Law as well.

However, the Great Assembly dissolved around 280 BC. Subsequently, until the Jews codified the oral tradition in writing, they carried forward the oral tradition using paired priests or the rabbis, who also served in a judicial and legislative function regarding the Law.

The lawyers (sometimes called scribes), priests, and certain Jewish sects (such as the Pharisees) studied every Old Testament book and the oral traditions for application of the law in a theocracy. The Jewish priests ruled Palestine as a theocracy even when Palestine was politically governed by the Seleucids (the descendants of one of Alexander's generals who ruled Syria and Palestine) and later under Herod and Rome. Of course, this odd political/religious relationship resulted in some conflict between the civil and religious authorities—for example, in the time of Jesus, the Jewish authorities did not have the authority to execute a man. Accordingly, the Sanhedrin (the Jewish ruling counsel) had to trump up some sedition charges against Jesus so that the Romans would execute Him; the Sanhedrin could not execute Him for what they considered blasphemy (that is, claiming to be the son of God) because the Romans reserved the rights of execution to themselves.

Since the Jews had only written down the Torah, the Mosaic Law, study included not only the in-depth learning of the written law but also involved memorization of the oral tradition, teaching by such scholars as Gamaliel, and debate. The Law, which for this purpose includes the oral tradition, evolved and expanded as various Jewish religious leaders found it necessary to interpret the law in connection with changing circumstances whether relating to cultural, religious, ethical, or business issues.

As we can see, the learning organization first created by Ezra changed in form over time, but the Jewish leaders were always very involved with its maintenance and continuance. Only with their continued involvement were Jewish core values and its core ideology maintained for 2,500 years—from Ezra until now—values and an ideology that could have been easily lost except for the revival under Ezra and his creation of a tradition relating to the Rabbinic literature.

Top management must learn from the lessons of the Jews and create their own learning organization (the organization that Senge suggests and the organization that the Jewish theocrats employed 2,500 years before Senge ever wrote about it). As mentioned previously, involvement by top management is essential for maintaining an organization that adapts and learns as circumstances change. Similarly, top management must stay involved to ensure that the company's core values and ideology are recognized, maintained, and even changed as circumstances dictate.

The Jewish leaders did provide for a flexible, learning organization. However, later Jewish leaders (such as the Pharisees) made the law inflexible and became involved in minutiae in its interpretation. This last point suggests that an organization should never be so immersed in its organizational paradigm, or model, that it develops rigor mortis of the brain. In other words, business must create a learning organization that understands that "Our ability to learn faster than our competitors may be the only sustainable competitive advantage."[19] This ability inherently requires flexibility and adaptability.

COACHING

Coaching involves selecting the best people for the right jobs. We should all have equal opportunities, but we all know that God gave us different talents. Coaches, the management of a company in this metaphor, should recognize those employees (or prospects) with the best talent and put them into the right position. In this area, we find Collins in *Good to Great* disagreeing with the conclusions of his first book, *Built to Last*. In the first book, he said that effectively led people were important to a company's success. In the second book, *Good to Great*, he modifies that conclusion by saying you need the *right* people to achieve success.

Of course, any long-time coach would have agreed with that second conclusion simply based on their experience in coaching. Coaching is just picking the right people to do the right job.

For example, a football coach does not place a tight end in the quarterback's job unless the tight end has the talents and skills required of a quarterback. Likewise, you do not waste a good salesman by creating a poor sales manager.

Moses selected effectively when he assigned leaders based on their qualifications, as Jethro suggested—Godly men, men of integrity, and men with leadership capabilities. Jesus also effectively selected his disciples—notice that Jesus many times simply told them to come follow Him and they did (that is without a contract, an office visit, or a signing bonus). Jesus even rejected some men that wanted to join Him because He knew that their hearts were not right. For example, the rich young ruler came to join Jesus, but when he was instructed to give up his wealth (the love of money surfaces) the young man left without joining. In another example, when a man said he wanted to be a disciple but needed to go home and bury his parents first, Jesus also rejected him because his priorities were not in the right order (see Matthew 8:21 to 8:22). Notice that Jesus even culled his disciples: in Mark 3 he selected twelve to serve as apostles, "...that he might send them out to preach and to have authority to drive out demons."[20]

Coaching also involves training. Any sports fan has witnessed the coaches on the sidelines or in the dugout constantly coaching the players. It is not so much an effort to tell them what they did wrong but more an effort to teach them how to do something right. So it was with Jesus in His teaching of His disciples—teaching that proved so effective that all of the disciples with the exception of John were martyred (quite a commitment).

When Jesus chose an apostle or when Paul chose another missionary, they always chose a person with temperament and acumen for the job. The exception is Judas, but God chose him to carry out a specific purpose, which was treachery, in order to achieve God's plan of salvation for the entire world.

Coaching also involves recognizing and developing raw talent. Peter, a fisherman, was an unlikely candidate for either discipleship or apostleship. However, Jesus recognized a tenacity and strength in Peter's character that overcame his relative lack of education. His strength of character, although previously weak at times, led this uneducated fisherman to travel to sophisticated, but pagan, Rome as a missionary and to stand up to the Sanhedrin when they told him to stop preaching and healing. Some Christians even consider Peter the first bishop of Rome.

Coaching in business requires recognizing that raw talent (the right person may have the talent but that right person may be undeveloped or immature) and instructing that talent in how and what he should do. Sometimes this requires the person to obtain more schooling or more experience. Regardless, if the person has the talent the company would prove unwise if it did not provide the person the opportunity.

Further, management should provide such opportunity and help without discrimination. Often those with a talent for leadership, for sales, and for administration have not received the proper training. As ACIPCO (more about this company in the fourth chapter) did in its early days and as many companies do today, companies should provide a hand up for those who need one. Isn't it better to create a productive and loyal employee through use of the Golden Rule (more about this in the next chapter) rather than an embittered one who knows his talents were ignored? Doesn't the Golden Rule mean to lean down and help somebody up?

Based on what you have previously read, you decide. However, perhaps you should wait and read the next chapter or the next before making that decision. Regardless, in a paraphrase of Joshua's great pledge (see Josh. 24:15), for my company and me, we will serve the Lord through helping, loving, and caring for His people.

FOOTNOTES

[1] Exod. 3:11 NIV.

[2] James C. Collins, *Good to Great: Why Some Companies Make the Leap and Others Don't* (New York: HarperBusiness, 2001), 36.

[3] Ibid. Collins uses the term "business" where the author has inserted institution. Regardless, a humble leader with a strong will should accomplish excellent results whatever his position.

[4] Ps. 8:4 NIV.

[5] William Barclay, *The Daily Bible Study Bible Series*, rev. ed., "The Gospel of Matthew, vol. 1 (Philadelphia: Westminster Press®, 1958), 98.

[6] Collins, 39.

[7] Collins, 37.

[8] 2 Tim. 1:12 NIV. The author means no disrespect to Dr. Collins, whom the author holds in the highest regard. For all the author knows (since the author does not know him), Dr. Collins may believe himself in the quoted verse from Timothy. The author only quibbles with the use of "might" when he knows that God "will" make a change in the life of a person who becomes born again.

[9] A Theory X manager is one that believes that management consists of coercion and driving workers. In contrast, a Theory Y manager believes in treating his employees right and providing them with incentives to do well.

[10] Numbers 1:44 NIV says that there were 603,550 men twenty years or older when the census in Numbers was taken. If we multiply that number for the approximate American family size, say 2.5, then the number of people would aggregate approximately 1.5 million, which is low because the Hebrews probably had a larger average family size. Regardless, we see that Moses had quite a task before him.

[11] Rom. 7:15 NIV.

[12] Peter M. Senge, *The Fifth Discipline, The Art & Practice of The Learning Organization* (New York: Currency Doubleday, 1990), 360.

[13] Mark 4:33-34 NIV.

14 Ezra 7:6 NIV.

15 Ibid.

16 Ezra 7:10 NIV.

17 God created these laws to prevent the syncretism of Judaism by the mixture of various pagan religions into Judaism. These laws did not relate to race, color, creed, or ethnicity.

18 Neh. 13:11 NIV.

19 Senge, 4.

20 Mark 3:14-15, NIV.

CHAPTER 3

WISDOM AND A
GOOD BOOK
LEADER

No leader, no matter how experienced or naturally gifted, can apply the leadership techniques discussed in the previous chapter without wisdom. Without this vital element, a leader will fail—no matter what business and management techniques he uses, what books he reads, or what seminars he attends.

But one can acquire wisdom if he is willing to listen and learn without letting ego get in his way. Accordingly, this chapter will explore the Good Book's concept of wisdom as an essential characteristic of an effective leader. We will see how it was demonstrated in the lives of Biblical leaders, and will draw conclusions from those examples.

EXAMPLES OF WISDOM

This book promotes the concept that even the egotistical may change and obtain humility by simply letting Jesus into their hearts (of course, they have to be humble enough to do so) because true Christians are by nature humble people. In addition, even the secular can learn humility by studying the Good Book or philosophy with humility at its core.

Further, anyone can learn to be wise so long as one learns to listen and study persistently without letting ego get into the way. Accordingly, this chapter talks about the Good Book's concept of wisdom—one of the essential characteristics of an effective leader.

SOLOMON

Solomon was purportedly one of the wisest men of all time. When he succeeded his father, David, as King of Israel, God offered Solomon a gift. God offered him the choice of anything he wanted without limit (1 Kings 3:5). Now, any other Middle Eastern king of that era—or for that matter probably any ruler or CEO of today—would have humanly and materialistically asked for money, longevity, land, other kingdoms (or, today, countries or companies), beautiful women, many children (or maybe not), military power, and military expertise.

Being a Middle Eastern king of the eleventh century BC, Solomon may have thought to ask for military power and prowess because with those two things he could have acquired everything else he would have otherwise desired. Note that David had acquired much of his power through military conquest—with the able help of Joab, his chief general, but primarily because God loved David.

Military power, the logistics to support an army, and military prowess would have allowed Solomon the opportunity to obtain further riches, land, and power through conquest. At that time, the entire Middle East was warlike— for example, Egypt and the Philistines to the South, the Hittites to the North, and Assyria to the Northeast, bordered Israel. Solomon would have understood that the way to grow a kingdom, or empire, was through the acquisition of other people's riches and territories by violent means.

Even today, many businesses use similar warlike techniques to grow—although the killing of others is left out (in most cases anyway). For example, the hostile takeover through acquisitions of other company's stock is by its nature a warlike technique. If offered a gift from God today, a CEO might ask for appropriate business acumen (or prowess) and business power to make the correct strategic acquisitions. The correct and strategic acquisition could then result in the multiplication of the CEO's and his business's riches and power.

However, Solomon did not ask for things that other rulers of his time, or even a celebrity CEO of today, might want. Rather, he asked for wisdom—the wisdom to govern and administer the people of Israel. Now wisdom is something that the humble CEO Collins discusses might value.

Wisdom is prowess—that is the ability to do something well. In addition, wisdom involves the ability to apply knowledge correctly, effectively, and strategically. By asking for wisdom, Solomon obtained the power and riches another person might have asked for, since power and riches can be obtained through the appropriate application of wisdom.

Perhaps, Solomon learned something from his dad. David had used his military prowess and the Lord's blessing to defeat the Philistines. He then expanded Israel to a size and strength that laid the foundation of Solomon's larger kingdom. Solomon understood that David, through the application of military wisdom, united a fractious and contentious people into a united kingdom (which unfortunately only stayed united through Solomon's reign—more about that later).

The Lord was so pleased with Solomon's request for wisdom that he granted him all the other things he did not ask for—that is, riches, land, glory, and honor. The Lord also conditionally granted Solomon longevity so long as he obeyed the Lord's laws and commandments (1 Kings 3:14). According to 1 Kings, Solomon's wisdom was greater than any other wise man of the time (1 Kings 4:29-31). From all of this we can see how much the Lord values wisdom.

God also extended to Solomon various abilities that require skill (that is, prowess) to apply them. For example, God granted Solomon the ability to write (Proverbs and Ecclesiastes are both attributed to Solomon), the skills of a biologist (1 Kings 4:33), and the proficiency of a botanist (1 Kings 4:33).

However, the most important ability God granted Solomon was the wisdom of administration: wisdom that he could use in administering his people and kingdom. Most business leaders of today also aspire to obtain that type of wisdom.

Solomon knew his people were contentious (just read the books of law, history, and the prophets for a history of a stubborn, touchy, ungrateful, quarrelling, and disloyal people—the Israelites). That is why Solomon asked for wisdom to govern. To wit: "So give your servant [i.e., Solomon] a discerning heart to govern your people and to distinguish between right and wrong. For who is able to govern this great people of yours?" (1 Kings 3:9) You would have to say that the Solomon's question was a very good one since the Lord himself through his servants Moses, Joshua, the judges, and even David had found the administration of the Israelites a daunting task. Today's managers often find themselves in the same boat as Solomon, facing tasks that are equally as daunting.

As we know from 1 Kings, Solomon used his wisdom to grow his kingdom and made Israel one of the strongest and most prosperous kingdoms in the Middle East at that time. This was difficult task in itself since the United Kingdom (what later became Judah and Israel when the United Kingdom divided during Rehoboam's reign) was surrounded by numerous unfriendly countries including Aram (now Syria), Edom (now part of Saudi Arabia), Ammon (now

Jordan), Moab (now part of Jordan), and Philistia (now southwest Israel and the Gaza Strip). The United Kingdom lay between the various empires of Mesopotamia (modern Iraq) and Persia (modern Iran) to the northeast and east, and the Egyptians to the southwest. The United Kingdom and its progeny (Israel and Judah) were the natural routes of conquest and war between the powers of Mesopotamia/Persia and Egypt. You could say that the main interstate (or autobahn) for moving troops between Asia Minor, Mesopotamia, and Egypt lay right in the middle of the United Kingdom.

Solomon also used his wisdom to build the temple, which required biblical, architectural, administrative, logistical, and engineering skills, and some strategic alliances, particularly with Hiram, the King of Tyre (a Phoenician city now located in modern Lebanon).

JOSEPH

Joseph, Jacob's beloved youngest son, offers another example. Joseph always displayed wisdom throughout his adversity in Egypt although he had to accumulate such wisdom the hard way. For you see, Joseph was initially unwise. As a young man, he was unwise enough to flaunt his father's love for him over his brothers, which was not exactly a good way for him to endear himself with his older brothers. (Nor was it wise for Jacob to flaunt his love of Joseph by honoring Joseph with a multi-colored coat.)[1]

Joseph also proved to be a tattletail (not an endearing trait) by telling his father, Jacob (also known as Israel), that his brothers had been doing something bad. We do not know exactly what, but we do know he brought a bad report to his father about them (See Gen 37:2). He also reported a dream that he would at sometime be lord over his brothers, which, again, his elder brothers did not appreciate. A wiser young man would have probably kept that dream to himself, given the state of his relationship with his brothers.

Joseph's dysfunctional relationship with his brothers finally got Joseph into trouble—trouble that subsequently would prove to his and their benefit—although Joseph probably did not feel that way at the time.

When Jacob later sent Joseph to check on his brothers who were in the Dothan countryside tending Jacob's flocks, the brothers decided to get even with the brother whom they both envied and disliked. When the brothers saw Joseph approaching them they decided to kill him on the spot. However, Joseph's eldest brother, Reuben, intervened and convinced the other brothers not to kill him, since he was, after all, their brother. Heeding Reuben's advice, the brothers, instead, threw him into an empty cistern.

When a caravan of Ishmaelites/Midianites happened by, Judah (another of Joseph's brothers) suggested to the other brothers that they accomplish two purposes by selling Joseph to the caravan's merchants. First, they could make some money, and second, they could get rid of Joseph.

To cover up their selling of Joseph to the traders, they went home and told Jacob that a wild animal had killed Joseph. In what probably seemed ironic to them, the brothers used Joseph's multi-colored coat to complete the deception by soaking the coat in blood so that it appeared an animal had indeed attacked Joseph.

The Midianite traders then took Joseph to Egypt and sold him as a slave to Potiphar, an important Egyptian official who served as the captain of Pharaoh's palace guard. Immediately upon becoming part of Potiphar's household, Joseph began exercising wisdom—something he had lacked when he had previously dealt with his brothers. Joseph's display of wisdom is even more remarkable when you consider his position as a slave within a foreigner's household. At that time, a slave was not highly regarded—that is, he was chattel: the personal property of his master. The master could do anything with a slave that he wished to do. As property, Joseph had no rights and served simply as a tool of his master. As a tool, Joseph's master could use Joseph to perform whatever menial task the master assigned him.[2]

Joseph, however, made the best he could of a bad situation and, instead of sulking or minimally performing his tasks, he made himself indispensable to Potiphar (which is again noteworthy since as a nomadic shepherd Joseph was probably uneducated and certainly did not know Egyptian). Regardless, he learned what he needed to know, which is wisdom in itself, and performed his tasks remarkably well, since, as the Good Book says, the Lord was with Joseph. He performed so well in fact that Potiphar made him the head of his household, second only to Potiphar and Potiphar's family.

Now how God gave Joseph success and how Joseph acquired the knowledge to run a wealthy Egyptian's household we do not really know. Nevertheless, we can surmise that Joseph used his acquired knowledge wisely to perform every task assigned to him in an exceptional manner—a manner not generally associated with a slave's performance—especially, an uneducated, Hebrew slave.

Later, as we know, Joseph got into trouble because of Potiphar's wife. Joseph did not create this trouble but inadvertently fell into it because of the lust of Potiphar's wife for him. Wisely, he rejected her advances but when scorned, she accused Joseph of rape.

Although the Bible does not state this (only saying that Potiphar "burned with anger," Gen 39:19), Potiphar probably did not completely believe his wife (or at least he had his doubts) because he did not have Joseph killed. If Potiphar had believed her (again this is just supposition), he could have easily had Joseph killed without consequence because he had the power to do so—both as a Joseph's master and an

Egyptian military official. However, as Joseph Heller called such a situation, Potiphar's wife had put Potiphar in a Catch-22. In other words, Potiphar's wife had placed Potiphar in an intractable situation where he had to do something even if he did not want to punish Joseph because he distrusted his wife. Potiphar had to punish Joseph, especially since Potiphar's wife had made sure that everyone in the house knew about the accusation.

Prison was the least of the punishments available, so Potiphar had Joseph thrown into prison.[3] But the Lord was with Joseph, and a term in prison was part of His ultimate plan to use Joseph as an instrument to save Jacob and his sons.

Again, Joseph performed well in a bad situation. In prison, because of his performance, Joseph came to the notice of what we would call the warden (called the "keeper of the prison" in the King James Version of the Bible). Ultimately, the warden put Joseph in charge of the prison and delegated the responsibility for all the prison to Joseph (again, he was in the number 2 position). The Bible goes on to say that the warden completely trusted Joseph's administration.

The Bible says that the warden was kind and gave Joseph authority over the prison because the Lord was with him. The Lord was with Joseph because he applied his God given skills and the wisdom he had acquired through God's providence. Because of this, Joseph succeeded in applying his administrative skills in an unlikely place—a prison. Joseph would use these administrative skills later on in a much higher position.

Joseph followed God's laws and continued to worship Him even when he could have easily abandoned Him, as people often do in difficult situations, believing that God had abandoned them. This was probably the wisest of all his decisions, demonstrating that faith in God can prove advantageous.

How did God directly help Joseph? Any answer to that

question would prove pure supposition because the Bible does not directly address what Joseph did in the prison—it largely and vaguely attributes Joseph's success to God being with Joseph. However, an effective modern executive (the analog being the warden in this case) generally rewards performance and the wise use of one's ability—the warden himself was wise by putting the right man in the right job. It, therefore, does make sense that the Lord's blessings came about through

a) Joseph's attitude, that is, displaying wisdom in making the best of a bad situation, and

b) using his God-given talents to the best of his abilities—in other words, applying good sense to the knowledge and abilities God had given him.

Nevertheless, there was something else besides fearing the Lord (which Scofield defines as reverential trust),[4] discovering God, and God awarding wisdom, knowledge, and understanding to Joseph. It is something that Joseph demonstrated in his dealing with Potiphar and the prison warden—that is, God shielded Joseph because he walked in absolute integrity in his dealing with both of the Egyptians.

In this regard, Joseph met all of the requirements of a recent book titled *Integrity* by a law professor named Stephen L. Carter. That is, Joseph learned right and wrong through discernment. Next, he acted upon what he learned, and lastly, he ultimately spoke about what he had learned (specifically to his brothers when they came to Egypt looking for grain during the famine that Pharaoh had dreamed about and that Joseph interpreted for him).

THE DEFINITION OF WISDOM

You have probably noticed in these examples that the words wisdom, skill, and prowess have been used interchangeably. Prowess, according to *The American Heritage College Dictionary*, means, "superior skill or ability" while, according to *The Encarta Dictionary*, wisdom means, "the knowledge and experience needed to make sensible decisions and judgments, or the good sense shown by the decisions and judgments made." Both words relate in this book to the application of knowledge. For you see, there is a difference between wisdom and knowledge.

Knowledge may mean that you know some area—such as the Bible, its places, dates, parables, people, and laws. However, knowledge does not necessarily mean that you know how to apply that scriptural knowledge to your everyday life or to your business. That is where wisdom (or prowess) comes in. Wisdom not only includes the knowledge necessary to perform some function or activity but also the ability to apply that knowledge appropriately in any given situation. Often, one only acquires wisdom through the school of hard knocks—that is, through experience.

As those in the military will tell you, wisdom often comes about only through OJT—that is, on-the-job training. In this regard, Joseph probably learned the most about wisdom through OJT. In contrast, Solomon was lucky because he did not have to learn administration and governing the hard way; rather God gave it to him, and he had observed his father, David, practicing it.

OBTAINING WISDOM

Wisdom is as important today as it was to Solomon and Joseph. Its manifestations and applications may be different, but it is essential in business in these critical areas of leadership:

- having the requisite management skills and knowledge
- having the wisdom to apply those management skills appropriately and adroitly
- having a proper code of ethics
- knowing how to deal with people
- having the strength to drive an organization in a search for excellent results
- knowing your personal strengths and weaknesses
- knowing how to set a company's strategic direction
- knowing how to set a company's core values and how to determine its core ideology
- knowing how to motivate people
- knowing how to gauge risk

You may acquire wisdom as a gift of God as Solomon did (a natural talent), by observation as Solomon did by observing his father David, or from the school of hard knocks as Joseph did. Every good or bad business decision you make as a businessman will depend on your wise or unwise application of the knowledge you have acquired.

Of course, the wise application of knowledge means that you have the basic knowledge beforehand, which means you need to study and learn from teachers. Beyond the basics you have to learn how to apply that obtained knowledge in real-life management decisions.

This means that if you are an experienced supervisor or manager, you need to mentor someone so they can learn how to apply the knowledge they have but also the wisdom and knowledge you have. For the novice, this means you need to find a mentor for the same reasons—in other words, so you can learn to apply what you know appropriately.

The warden and Potiphar were both mentors to Joseph as was David to Solomon—mentors such as these teach you and tell you what works and what does not work from their own experience. However, be careful that you gauge the advice of your mentor—sometimes his technical advice may prove to be on the money, while his wisdom regarding people may not be as good as yours. It takes experience to discern such a problem, so you may find it wise to test advice that you may not completely believe in or obtain advice from other managers or mentors. As they say, a little experimentation with firecrackers may prevent a big explosion with nitroglycerin.

You must also observe, as Solomon did with David and as Joseph probably did with Potiphar and the prison warden. As with the firecracker, observation may prevent you from creating a big mess. Observation often proves the best teacher because people sometimes do not do things exactly as they tell you they do them.

A wise mentor will start you off small and will allow you to grow into your position. The army does not make you the general in charge immediately (unless, of course, you are an Alexander and there was only one of him and, besides, he was taught by Aristotle), and neither should your company put you in a position you are not right or ready for. You should probably start out supervising a few people and then growing into more responsible positions as you demonstrate your readiness.

The mentor will allow you to make mistakes by allowing you to do things on a small scale so that you may learn without causing any harmful effects to your company. Although you may feel any mistakes you make at first are consequential, time will bring clarity to the magnitude of any mistakes you may make. You have to have room to make those small mistakes because that is how you become wise (please note this if you are a mentor).

Your mentor needs to determine whether you are the right person for the position from the beginning, assuming the mentor has no innate biases. For example, you may prove to be a skill person—a person who has certain knowledge and technical skills but who does not have the skills to be a leader. You may not be humble, you may not be strong, or you may not be dedicated. Regardless, your mentor should determine that and communicate it to you before you or the company gets into a position neither of you should be in. Remember that Jesus did not make every one of his disciples an apostle and not every chemist can become the plant manager of a chemical plant. A wise mentor, like a wise coach, will recognize your skill sets and not try to make quarterbacks out of skill players.

Becoming a leader means that you are willing to take the risks—by nature, the leader recognizes the risks and decides whether the group, company, or institution should take those risks or not. Taking and assessing risks involves a great deal of wisdom, which you can only learn patiently over time.

If you are not willing to make mistakes and take risks, you probably should not be in a leadership position. Those in leadership positions at your company, or your mentor, should recognize these weaknesses and not allow someone to become a leader if those people are risk adverse or poor judges of risk—after all, most business involves the assessment of risk and the taking of calculated risks. Solomon only expanded his empire by taking calculated risks as did his father, David, and history credits both as being great leaders.

The American philosopher George Santayana said, "Those who cannot remember the past are condemned to repeat it."[5] Accordingly, study your Bible and business history to learn "what is" and "what is not" foolishness—that is, anti-wisdom.

For example, 3,100 years ago Rehoboam became the king of the United Kingdom. This was a mistake of his culture because the eldest son became king regardless of his abilities, which, sadly, in some regards, Rehoboam lacked.

When the Israelites gathered at Shechem to make him King, they asked Rehoboam for some relief from the edicts of Solomon. Solomon, in his desire to build the temple, build a large palace for himself, and to build other things such as forts throughout the United Kingdom, required forced labor by the Israelites. The harshness of Solomon's forced labor, which the Israelites referred to as Solomon's "heavy yoke" (1 Kings 12 4), had been one of Solomon's unwise moves—despite his reputation for wisdom, he did make some unwise decisions.

Rehoboam told the people to go away for three days so he could make a decision concerning their request. He initially went to his father's advisors, who wisely told him to back away from the forced conscription policies of Solomon. However, Rehoboam did not heed their advice, since his father had not told him that he should do so, but, instead, went to some of his younger advisors for advice. This latter group, in a very unwise move, told Rehoboam to tell the people, essentially, that if they thought Solomon was bad, just wait. Rehoboam accepted the advice of his young advisors and told the people that his yoke would be even heavier than his father's yoke.

Naturally, the people were none too happy with this response and the ten northern tribes called on Jeroboam, who had returned from a self-imposed exile in Egypt, to become their king. This appointment of Jeroboam to the throne of the northern kingdom resulted in the split of the United Kingdom into two parts—Israel, the northern kingdom, and Judah, the southern kingdom.

Of course, not all the blame can go to Solomon. Rehoboam shares in the blame also because he obviously had not observed his father in action or learned from the man who was purportedly the wisest on earth at the time. Rehoboam also failed to respect the advice of his elders—a common occurrence in the Western world, where many think that youth is the only thing that matters.

However, Solomon also failed. A wiser man would have told Rehoboam of the potential problem and may have even tried to settle it before Rehoboam took over. A wiser King may have ignored the rule of primogeniture (succession by the eldest) and appointed a wise successor—many American CEOs often encounter this same problem when they fail to hire or appoint the right successor.

The point here is to study history. In particular, the recitation of recent business history is probably the best thing about the books written by Peters, Reichheld, Collins, Porras, and Senge.[6] That is, they talk about business history, specifically what companies did right and wrong.

In summary, we can tell you how to pursue wisdom, obtain knowledge, and perform certain management techniques to make you a better leader. However, we cannot tell you how to become a leader.

Leadership is not for everyone because it requires the constant pursuit of wisdom, an effort you may not be willing to make. In addition, God may not have given you the appropriate skills. Accordingly, as suggested above, perhaps the wisest course for you is to be happy with your skill player position and leave the quarterbacking to others. However, be wise enough to know if you are not qualified and do not let your company make its best salesman into its worse sales manager.

FOOTNOTES

[1] As you will remember, Jacob had sons by his two wives, Leah and Rachel, and their handmaidens, Bilhah and Zilpah. Rachel, however, was the most loved of his wives—he had only married Leah because of the trickery of his father-in-law, Laban.

[2] The HBO series called *Rome*, although both violent and lascivious, does provide insight into the use of slaves in the ancient world where they were used to such an extent that free man had no jobs. Slaves were also property that the Romans bought and sold at will. The Romans believed that slaves deserved to be slaves because they could have easily escaped slavery by killing themselves.

[3] In Proverbs 2:16 NIV, Solomon declares that wisdom will save you from the adulteress. The story of Joseph and Potiphar's wife is a perfect example of this truth.

[4] Scofield, Ps. 19:9, footnote 1, 550.

[5] William J. Federer, "George Santayana" in *Great Quotations : A Collection of Passages, Phrases, and Quotations Influencing Early and Modern World History Referenced according to their Sources in Literature, Memoirs, Letters, Governmental Documents, Speeches, Charters, Court Decisions and Constitutions* (St. Louis, MO: AmeriSearch, 2001).

[6] Interestingly, when the author attended a college of business, the college required no study of business history. In other words, we were free to make the same mistakes all over again—of course, our ignorance would not excuse our making them.

CHAPTER 4

YOUR MOST IMPORTANT ASSET

Collin and Porras point out in their book *Built to Last* that many successful companies list the care and loving management of their people as one of their core values. What surprises the author is that that's not the case with many companies.

When I asked fellow businessmen at a weekly prayer breakfast their opinions about a company's most important asset, the local owner of a large Birmingham machine shop, Bayliss Machine, readily and without hesitation replied, "People." Interestingly, what was common business sense for a local business owner has required many studies by both academics and consultants.

Unsurprisingly, academic studies have proven that people are more important than capital or products to the success of a company. Now if the academics had only studied the Bible first they would have found that God has always put people first and they could have, by doing so, avoided a lot of work and analysis (in the alternative, they could have simply asked the Meadow Brook Baptist Church Thursday morning prayer group).

This book will spend a lot of time discussing man's love of God and man's love of man because those two principles are the foundation of the Golden Rule. This well-known guideline has many business applications besides the proper treatment of your employees, many of which will be discussed in this book.

WHAT IS LOVE?

Before addressing the Golden Rule, you must first understand the meaning of the verb love, which God uses as an imperative in His Golden Rule. An imperative love means that God requires you to love others as He defines it. In other words, such love is not optional.

The English verb love means many things—some of which are ungodly and not neighborly. For example, *Webster's* defines love as follows:

> transitive verb
> 1 : to hold dear : cherish
> 2 a : to feel a lover's passion, devotion, or tenderness for
> 2 b (1) : caress
> (2) : to fondle amorously
> (3) : to copulate with
> 3 : to like or desire actively : take pleasure in (loved to play the violin)
> 4 : to thrive in (the rose loves sunlight)
> intransitive verb
> : to feel affection or experience desire[1]

From those definitions, you can see that in English, the verb love conveys different meanings. For example, we use love in the following ways:

- I love Armour hot dogs.
- I love to go fishing.
- I love baseball.

- I love you.
- I love my children.
- I love my brother.
- I love my church.
- I love New York (well, at least some people do).

The New Testament writers used Koine Greek (the common pidgin Greek used in Western Civilization at the time) in composing the New Testament. It does not suffer from English's general definitional limitations with regard to the verb love. In fact, Koine Greek has several verbs that one can translate into the English verb love. Those Greek verbs include agapao, eros, phileo, or epithumeo all which involve an action—the requirement of a verb.

Agápe love is the type of love that Jesus refers to in Matthew 22:39 and following, where He identifies God's two greatest commandments. Eros refers to romantic or sensual love, and according to *Harper's Bible Dictionary* does not appear in the New Testament. Phileo refers to affection for something or some person. Epithumeo means to desire something. Generally, in the New Testament interpreters translate the verbs agapao or phileo as the English verb love.

The Greeks often combined the noun form of one of their love verbs with another noun to create a new noun. For example, the Greeks used phileo to produce such nouns as philanthropia (modern philanthropy, love of men—where anthropos is the Greek word for man), philadelphia (brotherly love, which William Penn used in naming Philadelphia, Pennsylvania), and philarguria (the love of money, which in the New Testament is often referred to as a sin).[2] As you can see from such noun usage, one finds phileo used in the sense of "affection for" or as Webster connotes "to hold dear."

Nevertheless, Jesus deliberately chose the word agapao

rather than phileo to express the love you should show for one another ("Love your neighbor as yourself," Matt. 22:39 NIV) and this word does not denote affection. Agapao connotes a deep love for another—this is not love in a familial or a sensual way, but love in the way God loves humanity. God expressed His agápe love by sending His Son to die on the cross at Calvary for the collective sins of humanity. This agápe love, displayed through Jesus' sacrifice, allows mankind to live more abundantly and with a greater purpose.

THE PRACTICE OF LOVE

A Jewish lawyer (also called a scribe) asked Jesus, "What is the greatest commandment?"[3] As lawyers do, the lawyer used a question "what is the greatest commandment" to test Jesus' knowledge of the law and discredit Him if possible. As you are aware, lawyers in our time, in direct or cross-examination, ask a witness questions, and then attempt to use the witness's answers to discredit the witness or his testimony. The lawyer, here, had the same motive.

Indeed, Jesus served as a witness of God's love and God's teachings—teachings that did not fall in line with those of the scribes and Pharisees. It is easy to suppose that the lawyer thought he could readily discredit an uneducated, itinerant preacher from Nazareth whose primary occupation was carpentry.

Although the lawyer's motive amounts to a supposition, the Pharisees and scribes constantly attempted to discredit Jesus before His followers: accordingly, the supposition falls in line with the behavior of the scribes and Pharisees in other parts of the Gospels. The lawyer probably wanted a response that he could use to display Jesus' ignorance or to illustrate His misinterpretation of the law.

The lawyer may have even expected a very complex reply because that is probably how he would have replied. He probably even hoped for a complex answer because he, then, could have more completely interrogated Jesus and attacked Jesus' answers. In other words, he probably hoped that Jesus' reply would allow further cross-examination and an opportunity to show the people how wrong the teachings of Jesus were.

However, Jesus did not provide a discourse on the Law or its oral traditions. Rather, He replied succinctly in only four verses containing forty-eight words. As you know, a person who can succinctly explain a complex concept demonstrates a complete grasp and understanding of the subject.

It was so with Jesus. He provided a simple and complete answer that probably surprised and discomfited the lawyer, offering no chance for rebuttal because of Jesus' understanding and mastery of the law and scripture—pretty good for a carpenter from Nazareth.[4]

Interestingly, Jesus did not answer with one commandment but with two. He expanded slightly because He understood that the first commandment leads to the second and that the two commandments are interlinked— that is, one goes with the other. Jesus, in reply to the lawyer's question, said:

> "Love the Lord your God with all your heart and with all your soul and with all your mind." This is the first and greatest commandment. And the second is like it: "Love your neighbor as yourself." *All the Law* and the Prophets hang on these two commandments. [Footnotes and verses omitted.] [Emphasis added.][5]

Neither of the commandments named by Jesus comes from the Ten Commandments. For example, neither the Ten Commandments located at Exodus 20 nor the Ten Commandments located at Deuteronomy 5 contains either one.[6]

The first commandment Jesus quoted, "Love the Lord your God with all your heart and with all your soul and with all your strength,"[7] comes from Deuteronomy 6:4-5.

The second commandment Jesus quoted comes from a phrase contained in Leviticus 19:18: "Do not seek revenge or bear a grudge against one of your people, but *love your neighbor as yourself*. I am the Lord."[8] [Emphasis added.] Generally, this means to do unto others as you would have them do unto you (see Matthew 7:12) and people usually refer to it as the Golden Rule. The biblical Golden Rule contrasts sharply with such non-Christian rules like:

> "He who has the gold makes the rules"; or
> "Do unto others before they do unto you" (in
> the sense that you do something bad to
> someone else before they have a chance to
> do something bad to you).

LOVE OF GOD

Many say that to love God, you must fear Him. However, this does not mean to dread Him. Rather, it means to revere Him.

For example, *The Holy Bible: The Good News Translation* translates fear as reverence ("To have knowledge, you must first have reverence for the Lord.").[9] Accordingly, you must acknowledge God and His power and His holiness and His love (John 3:16) before you can come to love Him. Once you acknowledge God, you should also come to love Him (unfortunately, as described afterwards, acknowledgment does not always translate into love).

Once one truly loves God, then a change comes upon that person. This generally involves a turning around by the person. The Greek verb metanoia (which biblical interpreters often translate as repentance) connotes such a turning around—that is, a change in direction of one's life. That is, you turn from following your selfish desires and turn to following God's precepts and doing His work.

Acknowledgment of the Lord, however, does not necessarily result in a love of Him. For example, the devil acknowledges God and His power and fears Him. However, the devil rejected God's love and, because of that rejection, God ejected him from heaven.

Men also may acknowledge God but may not accept or love Him. The outreach program, Evangelism Explosion, refers to the acknowledgment of God without love as "intellectual assent." Intellectual assent does not amount to loving God and having Him in your heart. Rather, it amounts to deism, which is not love of God, but an acknowledgment of a supreme being.

The apostle James, in referring to doing God's work (see James 1:22-25), uses the imperatives "do" and "do not" to emphasize how you should follow God. In other words, do not just intellectually acknowledge the Bible (the "word") but do what the Bible says to do and what the Lord directs you to do through the indwelling Holy Spirit. James specifically said:

> Do not merely listen to the word, and so
> deceive yourselves. Do what it says. Anyone
> who listens to the word but does not do what
> it says is like a man who looks at his face in a
> mirror and, after looking at himself, goes
> away and immediately forgets what he looks
> like. But the man who looks intently into the

perfect law that gives freedom, and continues
to do this, not forgetting what he has heard,
but doing it—he will be blessed in what he
does.[10] [Verse numbers omitted and emphasis
added.]

Once you acknowledge God and accept Jesus into your
heart, the Holy Spirit enters you and fills an empty spot
within you that God left specifically for "It" to enter. Upon
accepting Jesus, you will want to do what God wants you to
do and the Holy Spirit, since "It" resides within you, will
constantly remind you to do so.

Similarly, upon accepting Jesus, you will wish to study His
word (yes, even Leviticus, Deuteronomy, Numbers, and
Jeremiah). You will find in your study of scripture what He
wants you to do and what He does not want you to do.

The acceptance of God does not necessarily mean that
you will become perfect ("for all have sinned and fall short of
the glory of God"[11])—the only person who never sinned was
Jesus. Even Paul, who suffered much in his service to the Lord
and his evangelism for Jesus Christ, declared that he was first
among sinners (see 1 Timothy 1:16—the NIV uses the word
"worst" rather than first). However, Paul repented (remember
metanoia—he turned his life around), as you should, and kept
doing God's will to the extent that, as a human, he could.

Our own sinful nature likes to pop out now and again
even if the Holy Spirit tells us otherwise. Even the apostle
Paul acknowledged that problem to his student Timothy.
Charles Dickens, in a letter to this son, said this about the
Golden Rule and applying it: "Try to do to others as you
would like to have them do to you; and do not be discouraged
if they fail sometimes. It is much better for you that they
should fail in obeying the greatest rule laid down by our
Saviour [sic] than that you should."[12]

There is no doubt that Paul loved God—he suffered as

much through his service to God as probably any man and was martyred for his service to God by the Romans. Although Paul first mistakenly tried to find God through obedience to the law as a Pharisee and as a persecutor of Christians, Jesus ultimately found Paul on the Damascus Road and turned him around. After the Damascus Road experience, Paul was forever changed and his actions in evangelizing most of the Greek and Roman world demonstrated that complete change and turn around in his life.

Paul found grace (sometimes defined as God's unmerited favor), and afterwards he went out and preached it throughout Asia Minor, Phoenicia, Syria, Palestine, Greece, and Rome. The grace that Paul talked about, taught, and spread throughout the Greek and Roman world is not just God's unmerited favor but God's unmerited love for sinful mankind ("what is man that you are mindful of him...?"[13]).

Paul taught that grace comes freely from God and does not involve anything we can do ourselves—that is where grace differs from the law, which is performance oriented. You cannot perform every tittle of the law—it is impossible to completely follow the law, and even one failure means complete failure (for by God's grace are you saved through faith and not by your works, lest any man should boast [the author's paraphrase], see Ephesians 2:8-9[14]).

However, failure does not nullify God's grace. Grace only means accepting a gift (a gift by definition is free) from God and loving Him, which Jesus said is the first and greatest commandment.

Loving God is the first and greatest commandment because it results from the acceptance of God's grace and results in what Jesus described to Nicodemus (see John 3:3) as being born again. Being born again just means making a complete turn-around in your life and becoming a new person—a person dedicated to the Lord, but one that still fails Him on occasion.[15]

LOVE OF MAN

So after you love God, what happens next? Well, you then begin loving people. Jesus said that loving people ranks as the second greatest commandment and that upon such love God founded all the law and the prophets (see Matthew 22:40). So, if you are going to love people according to the Good Book, you first must love God. Likewise, it follows that to love your employees you must first love God.

Loving man means that you:

1. Put your neighbor first in your dealings with him.
2. Always treat your neighbor as if you were his fiduciary—that is, with complete trust and fidelity.
3. Do what is best in the circumstances for your neighbor.
4. Forgive your neighbor when he fails you (see Matthew 6:15).
5. Aid your neighbor when he needs aid.
6. Pick your neighbor up when he falls.
7. Act as if you and your neighbor share the same race or ethnicity.
8. Teach your neighbor when he needs teaching.
9. Listen when he needs someone to listen.
10. Be there when your neighbor is sick or injured.
11. Assist your neighbor's family if he cannot do so.
12. Feed your neighbor if he cannot feed himself.
13. Give your neighbor sustaining drink when he is thirsty.

14. Pray for your neighbor when he asks for prayer or when you recognize his need for prayer.
15. Ask for his forgiveness when you fail your neighbor or his family.
16. Do not slander or libel your neighbor.
17. Do not envy your neighbor or covet what he owns.
18. Treat your neighbor fairly in all business dealing.
19. Hold your neighbor's confidences in secret.
20. Understand that your neighbor is as human as you are.
21. Receive your neighbor's justifiable criticism of you without defense.
22. Learn the good things your neighbor has to teach you.
23. Listen to your neighbor's spiritual teachings with objectivity and tolerance.
24. Provide your neighbor the time he needs from or with you.
25. Do not hold grudges against your neighbor.
26. Do not judge your neighbor (Matthew 7:1).
27. Love your neighbor just as God loves you.

Of course, you could easily add to this list (for example, "Love means never having to say you're sorry"—remember the movie *Love Story* starring Ali McGraw and Ryan O'Neal).[16] Nevertheless, one example of Jesus' love readily comes to mind as an illustration of His agápe principles.

LOVE OF NEIGHBORS[17]

In the gospel of Luke, the lawyer asks, "What must I do to inherit eternal life?"[18] instead of the question, asked in Mark and Matthew, "What is the greatest commandment?" In Luke, Jesus turned the question around and asked the lawyer how he understood the law. The lawyer replied with essentially the same answer as the one Jesus provided in Matthew and Mark, and Jesus accepted that answer as correct.

However, the lawyer in Luke, in order "to justify himself...", asked Jesus, "And who is my neighbor?"[19] To this question, Jesus recounted the story of the Good Samaritan.

In His story (or parable, if you will), Jesus told the story of a man who was injured and robbed and left lying beside a road. Some people walked by but avoided the injured man and did nothing to help him. The people walking by included a priest and a Levite—both supposedly religious men who should have understood the law's injunctions, but who avoided the man nonetheless.[20]

However, a Samaritan stopped by, helped the man, took him to an inn, and gave the innkeeper money to take care of the man until he recovered. Obviously, the injured man was the neighbor, and the Samaritan, the man obeying the Golden Rule (that is, the second greatest commandment according to Jesus in Matthew 22:39, Mark 12:31, and by the lawyer in Luke 10:27).

What is ironic in this incident is who loved his neighbor as himself (Matt. 22:39). The irony involves the person who did his duty in contrast to those who should have known better—the priest and the Levite.

Although we may not understand the historical significance, since "Good Samaritan" has carried over into English as an aphorism for someone who takes care of others, the Jewish people discriminated against the Samaritans and were prejudiced in their beliefs about them.

To make matters worse, the Samaritans did not follow the laws of the Jews but looked primarily to the Pentateuch (the five books of the law) as their scripture. In addition, they created their own temple on Mount Gerizim, where they continued to worship even after Hyrcanus[21] destroyed their temple in 109 BC.

Therefore, Jesus purposely used a person in His parable that the Jews hated and disdained because of his ethnic heritage and religion. In so doing, He illustrated that both the injured man and the Samaritan were neighbors even though a devout Jew would have had nothing to do with a Samaritan—not only because of a Jew's ethnic and religious heritage but also because Jews considered Samaritans "unclean." As you remember from Leviticus, there are many rules contained in the law concerning uncleanness and associating with people that were unclean (see Lev 11-15).

So, your neighbor is any person regardless of their religion, race, ethnicity, color, heritage, or livelihood. By that definition, your neighbor includes your employees and those that work under your supervision.

Of course, as demonstrated in the chapter on ethics, altruism expressed through the application of loving principles to your employees will produce positive business benefits. Books such as these listed below in one way or another describe what caring for, encouraging, teaching, and lifting up employees will do for a business.

- *Built to Last, Successful Habits of Visionary Companies*
- *The Fifth Discipline, The Art and Practice of The Learning Organization*
- *In Search of Excellence, Lessons from America's Best-Run Companies*
- *Nuts!, Southwest Airlines' Crazy Recipe for Business and Personal Success*

- *The Loyalty Effect, The Hidden Force Behind Growth, Profits, and Lasting Value*
- *Good to Great, Why Some Companies Make the Leap and Others Don't*
- all of Covey's books

All these effects are positive and include such things as reduced union grievances, greater efficiency, higher productivity, happier work environments, increased employee sales, higher participation in product design, and better customer service. Regardless of the benefits coming from effective management of a company's employees, the best book for learning how to care for, manage, and love your employees happens to be the oldest of the management books—that is, the Holy Bible.

The Bible acknowledges that man is selfish—"for all have sinned…" (Romans 3:23 NIV). Man has been selfish since the Garden of Eden. The Hebrews of the Exodus and those living afterwards displayed so much selfishness that Moses, the Prophets, and the Kings constantly had to ask God for forgiveness on their behalf since He constantly threatened to destroy the Israelites because of their inconstancy and apostasy.

We know that God never intended to destroy the Hebrews in His divine providence. He only threatened their annihilation so that Moses, the Prophets, the people, and the Kings would learn their need for repentance and their need for God.

Paradoxically, the Golden Rule does play to our selfishness. When the Golden Rule results in good for us and others, it cannot be bad. However, you should beware of situational ethics where good outcomes are justified, even when the method of getting there is entirely bad.

In regards to selfishness, we all want recognition and desire others to view us as winners. Maslowe in his hierarchy of needs suggests that such selfish needs become important to us after we satisfy our basic primal needs for food, shelter, and procreation.

Peters and Waterman point out that by using positive reinforcement and other motivational techniques, we can increase productivity by satisfying those selfish needs for recognition and winning.[22] Some would just call that common sense application of the Golden Rule and treating our neighbor in the manner we want to be treated. It results in participants becoming recognized winners.[23]

Rationalists such as Sam Harris, the author of *The End of Faith*, also find the Golden Rule effective from a selfish viewpoint. He says:

> To treat others ethically is to act out of concern for their happiness and suffering. It is, as Kant observed, to treat them as ends to themselves rather than as a means to some further end. Many ethical injunctions converge here—Kant's categorical imperative, Jesus' golden rule—but the basic facts are these: we experience happiness and suffering ourselves; we encounter others in the world and recognize that they experience happiness and suffering as well; we soon discover that "love" is largely a matter of wishing that others experience happiness rather than suffering; and most of us come to feel that love is more conducive to happiness, both our own and that of others, than hate. There is a circle here that links us to one another: we each want to be happy; the social feeling of love is one of our greatest sources of happiness; and love entails that we be concerned for the happiness of others. We discover that we can be selfish together.[24]

Regardless, the biblical love of neighbor comes from God's unselfish desire for the well-being of mankind. That is what He wants you to feel also, and that is why His scripture uses the Greek verb agapao for unselfish love in His command for us to love one another.

JESUS' LOVE OF SINNERS

God demonstrated His love for man in many examples throughout the Bible. He brought a disagreeable and undisciplined people out of Exodus and provided them with the Promised Land—a land flowing with milk and honey. Ultimately, He loved the world so completely that He sent His Son to die on the cross for the sins of mankind.

While Jesus was on earth, He showed His love of sinners in many very practical ways. For example, He called one tax collector, Matthew, to His direct service as a disciple (see Matthew 9:9) and forgave another, Zacchaeus (see Luke 19).

Today, you probably find it hard to understand the magnitude and meaning of Jesus' dealings with tax collectors—especially for a rabbi (or teacher) like Jesus to have dealings with a tax collector. Today, almost every businessman amounts to a tax collector—generally, every time you go to the grocery store, a pharmacy, or a restaurant,[25] or any type of retail establishment, you pay a sales tax (with certain state and/or local exceptions). If you drive, you pay a gasoline tax that the government includes within the sales price. If you work, you pay an income tax—at least at the federal level (there are certain state exceptions). If you own a home, you pay property taxes. If you own a car, you pay personal property taxes. Even if you die and your estate exceeds certain monetary limits, your estate pays taxes, at least at the federal level, on wealth that you accumulated during your lifetime using income that you had already paid taxes on—to paraphrase Professor Lane, a former tax professor at the University of Alabama, "You can not escape taxes even in death."

Regardless, people of today have generally resigned themselves to the payment of taxes. Although the people, depending on the government, may have the opportunity to ease the burden through a direct vote or a proposition, there is still little they can do to avoid the plethora of taxes common to the modern world.

However, in the Roman world, the people had no say in taxes—an imperial bureaucracy set them. The Jewish people did not like those imperial taxes, in particular, because Rome, an occupying power, assessed the various taxes depending on what they needed from occupied Palestine. Although Rome assessed the taxes, it used agents to collect them. These agents in occupied Palestine were the Jewish tax collectors to whom Jesus reached out.

Not only were the tax collectors agents of a hated occupying power—Rome—but the tax collectors made their money through commissions. They received a stated percentage of the collections, and if they collected more than they needed to collect, then they kept the excess. In other words, the tax collectors engaged in extortion with their own people. Because of this extortion, the tax collectors were relatively wealthy and the Jews, understandably, generally hated them.

The scribes and Pharisees hated the tax collectors because they violated God's law, which provides that one should not take advantage of the poor and needy (see Isaiah 10:1-3).[26] Rather, God's law (which ironically comes from the supposedly wrathful and vengeful Old Testament God) provides that the Jews should take care of the poor, which of course they failed to do. But who are we to point fingers when we do no better?

After the call of Matthew, Jesus went to his house and had dinner. Not surprisingly, many of the dinner guests were other tax collectors and, guess what, other "sinners"—if you were a tax collector, it was difficult to make friends with anyone other than another tax collector like yourself or other sinners. This was obviously bad, at least in the eyes of the scribes (lawyers) and Pharisees (a strict right-wing Jewish sect—probably like some current fundamentalist leaders in temperament, tolerance, and belief). For you see, a Rabbi, such as Jesus, should have avoided any contact with such sinners. Consequently, the Pharisees asked Jesus about His association with tax collectors and other sinners and said to Jesus, "What are you doing eating with sinners and tax collectors?" [Author's paraphrase.]

Jesus responded with a classic agápe response: "It is the sick that need a doctor not the healthy. I was called to reach out to sinners." [Author's paraphrase, see Matthew 9:12-13.] In other words, Jesus came to save the lost and what better place to reach sinners than a dinner filled with them. Now, a wrathful God would have found those sinners disgusting but a loving God saw that they needed help. Of course, Jesus' reply displeased the scribes and Pharisees because, for all their knowledge of the law, they had misunderstood its essence.

DISCRIMINATION

Before going further, this book needs to address the issue of discrimination because love of your neighbor includes everyone. That is, as an owner or manager of a company, you should treat everyone of your employees or subordinates equally, and should provide equal opportunity for each because God requires it.

Of course, there are many laws that require employers, and their officers and managers, to provide such non-discriminatory treatment to their employees or potential employees. Regardless, an owner or manager should practice non-discrimination because it is the right thing to do, not only because it is legally required.

Non-discrimination creates the type of loyalty that Reichheld suggests improves worker retention, boosts productivity, and results in higher profits. It should engender in the employee what Covey calls a win-win response. This type of loyalty increases employee involvement in all of the company's processes and reduces conflict between a company and its employees.

Nonetheless, this book, as supported by scripture, emphasizes that God's prescribed treatment of your neighbor *does not involve discrimination in any way.* God loves all humanity regardless of race, tribe, color, ethnicity, gender, mixture, or national origin. In other words, God does not see people as we sinful humans might but as His creation. How can He discriminate against His own sons and daughters?

Discrimination or discriminatory practices of whatever impact are *wrong and contrary to God's word and His love for humanity*—period, end of story. In support, St. Paul in his letter to the Galatians, said:

> You are *all* sons[27] [and daughters] of God through faith in Christ Jesus, for *all* of you who were baptized into Christ have clothed yourselves with Christ. There is *neither Jew nor Greek, slave nor free, male nor female, for all are one in Christ Jesus.* If you belong to Christ, then you are Abraham's seed, and heirs according to the promise. [Emphasis added, verses references omitted, and insert made by author.]

In a paraphrase of "Jesus Loves the Little Children," *we are all equal in his sight.*

God is the founder of anti-discrimination and the word discrimination was not in His lexicon before sinful man created, as he is wont to do, this evil. Only the devil could have caused man to devise a need for such an egregious cultural artifact—an artifact used to justify the worst sins of mankind—including slavery, intolerance, religious persecution, and genocide. No doubt the devil, as with Adam and Eve, used a very sublime and devious stratagem to divide and corrupt mankind and to lead man to the invention of such a blatantly evil concept.

Discrimination toward others and the hatred of those different from us should not be in a Christian's mindset, although discrimination by Christians has been commonplace throughout the centuries even toward other Christians— witness the inquisitions in Spain and Italy, and the killing of Protestants and Catholics during the Protestant Reformation. We only have to look at the previous century and our own to see such discrimination—some of which the discriminators support by open misinterpretation of scripture and a non-holistic approach to the Bible's overall teachings.

Regardless, whatever method or event the devil used to create man's discriminatory tendencies, discrimination truly meets the definition of evil and, unfortunately, the devil was truly successful in making such discrimination ubiquitous. In this regard, Carter in *Integrity*[28] states that the greatest consequence of the sin of discrimination[29] is genocide, which most men find extremely evil.

Discrimination is also unwise because it fosters all types of sin and evil:

- hate
- violence
- unfairness
- disunity
- poverty
- ignorance
- disease

All of these evils, whether societal, religious, or economic, are unwise to both those who study the Good Book and those who want to use its precepts in good business. All discrimination harms society and business as well—after all good business flourishes in a non-discriminatory, open, non-biased society.

However, for further proof, one need only study the core ideologies and core values of those companies studied by Collins and Porras in *Built to Last, Successful Habits of Visionary Companies*, Collins in *Good to Great, Why Some Companies Make the Leap and Others Don't*, and Peters and Waterman, *In Search of Excellence, Lessons from America's Best-Run Companies*. All three books emphasize people management and their involvement in the business process. Involvement of people in the management of a company for success is inherently non-discriminatory.

A Scriptural Example of Non-discrimination

Jesus emphasized the non-exclusivity of the Golden Rule and non-discrimination in His discussions with the Samaritan woman in John 4, and His subsequent evangelism of the local Samaritan populace.

As Jesus and the disciples traveled through Samaria, they stopped at a well. The disciples went from the well to find food, but Jesus stayed there and rested. A Samaritan woman came up, and Jesus asked her for a drink of water. We, of course, would not find this noteworthy unless we understand the societal implications of Jesus, a Jewish Rabbi, talking to a Samaritan woman.

You will remember that after Solomon's death, ten tribes rejected the rule of his son, Rehoboam, and formed the northern kingdom, Israel. Jeroboam initially ruled Israel, and

Rehoboam initially ruled the southern kingdom, Judah. Judah consisted of the tribe of Judah and the tribe of Benjamin.

The Assyrians conquered Israel in the eighth century BC. The Assyrians, to discourage revolt, often dispersed the people of a conquered nation. In Israel, the Assyrians used that method and dispersed some of the Jewish people, left a remnant, and moved some other conquered peoples into the former kingdom of Israel. This movement of peoples resulted in a mixed race as the Jewish remnant and the new immigrants intermarried—the Samaritans. The purebred Jewish people looked down upon this mixed race as mongrels and discriminated against them because of it. For example, the Jews did not allow the Samaritans to worship in the Temple at Jerusalem and the Jews treated the Samaritans as unclean.

The Jews also made it their practice to not associate with the Samaritans if they could avoid it. For instance, a devout Jew would not travel through Samaria but would take an alternate route even if that meant traveling a greater distance.

In contrast, here you have a Jewish rabbi, Jesus, talking to a Samaritan woman—someone the scribes and Pharisees would have avoided as we would avoid someone with either SARS or the Avian flu. Not only was the woman a disdained Samaritan, but she was also an adulteress several times over— a violation of the seventh commandment and the Levitical and Deuteronomic laws as well.

None of the Samaritan woman's characteristics bothered Jesus. Rather, He reached out to the woman and her people by preaching and teaching in her town for two days. Consequently, "…many more became believers."[30]

In reaching out to a Samaritan disdained by the Jewish religion, Jesus set the example of non-discrimination for all of us to follow. Often, those who have felt the brunt of discrimination are those in the most need of help—here Jesus demonstrated that principle by helping those who were in need of His help and His love.

Jesus also emphasized agápe love and its non-exclusivity when He preached the Sermon on the Mount (see Matt. 5-7 and Luke 6) to those who were following Him and looking for spiritual solace. In the Sermon on the Mount, Jesus said to love others even those that are different from you—even your enemies. Jesus specifically said:

> If you love those who love you, what credit is that to you? Even "sinners" love those who love them. And if you do good to those who are good to you, what credit is that to you? Even "sinners" do that. And if you lend to those from whom you expect repayment, what credit is that to you? Even "sinners" lend to "sinners," expecting to be repaid in full. But love your enemies, do good to them, and lend to them without expecting to get anything back. Then your reward will be great, and you will be sons of the Most High, because he is kind to the ungrateful and wicked. Be merciful, just as your Father is merciful.[31] [Verse numbers omitted.]

With that, anything else on the subject would amount to mere commentary.

MANAGING PEOPLE

While researching material for this book, I found that a union employee had written a poem about his employer's treatment of him at the plant where he worked. In that poem, the employee indicated that, although he was an adult and treated as an adult outside his working environment, his employer did not treat him so. This non-adult treatment occurred, according to the poet/employee, as soon as he entered his working environment—in other words, as soon as he stepped through the plant's gates.

Obviously, management of that plant applied classic Theory X management techniques, methods somewhat akin to what the Egyptians used to get the Hebrews to make bricks—that is, you drive people to work through coercion. Obviously, modern Theory X managers do not use whips—we are, after all, too civilized for such cruelty. Or, are we?

A Theory X manager believes you must maintain tight control and must strictly monitor your employees or subordinates. In the mind of a Theory X manager, you must constantly control and monitor employees because they are inherently lazy, dishonest, disruptive, and incompetent.

In contrast, a Theory Y employer applies the principles of the Good Book. The Theory Y employer, accordingly, treats employees as the adults they are.

Theory Y (perhaps someone will sometime in the future label it Theory J after Jesus) is how Jesus talked to people. Although, as a teacher, Jesus used stories and examples that the people would understand, He always treated His disciples and followers as adults. When Jesus spoke to people, He spoke to them directly with a spirit of wisdom and love. Why else do you think people followed an itinerant, impoverished preacher?

He must have had a tremendous amount of God-given charisma, the likes of which the world has not seen since.

Cynics might say that the people followed Him because He performed miracles, healed people, and provided free lunches, but many Israelites hated Him for doing such things. Others believe that He was charismatic, friendly, personable, and perfectly good. Many were attracted to Him, including

His disciples and the apostles, because He was perfect and they could see love in His every action.

In contrast, the religious leaders of His day (the members of the Sanhedrin, the scribes, and the Pharisees) did not display such love. Rather, we know that they were Theory X leaders because they were all too concerned with the rules Jesus and His followers might be breaking—such as healing on the Sabbath, a major breach of the Law in their minds—forgetting that God, after all, is love.

A Man God Has to Love

In recent history, there was a man who displayed the love Jesus expected a businessman to show. History has hidden him in the background and, therefore, you probably have not heard of him. Regardless, this man, before many of the good management theories came about or management consultants or academics espoused them, cared for his workers, understood their importance, and trained them well. This man did this by applying the Golden Rule in his company and in his dealing with his employees.

In the early twentieth century, a religious man named John H. Eagan founded a company best known by its acronym, ACIPCO (that is, American Cast Iron Pipe Company) in Birmingham, Alabama. Eagan based his management philosophy on one core value—the Golden Rule. In fact, belief in that core value continues today at ACIPCO.

For example, visitors to ACIPCO's web site are greeted with a message that reads, "100 Years of Proof That the Golden Rule Works."[32] To learn more about this history, you must first click a pop-up box. The underlying web script then takes you directly to a page that displays the Golden Rule from Matt. 7:12 verbatim—just in case you have forgotten the Golden Rule or never knew what it said in the first place.

Eagan practiced the Golden Rule at ACIPCO by doing such things as:

- providing pasture for the employee's cattle (not much of fringe benefit today but obviously one in the early twentieth century)
- creating a nine-hour work day (something not done in the age of worker exploitation in the early twentieth century)
- creating vacation and sick leave time
- creating employee Bible study groups
- supporting an Afro-American church (remember this was in Birmingham during the 1920s)
- supporting the YMCA
- providing worker training at night
- paying bonuses to hourly employees
- providing on-site healthcare
- providing a pension and insurance plan for all employees
- offering garden plots to employees during World War I because of food inflation

Amazingly, this culture of the Golden Rule continues after one hundred years of business operations. For example, *Fortune* has named ACIPCO to its 100 Best Companies to Work for List since the list's inception.

Mr. Eagan also did something that is almost unheard of—both now and then. Upon his death in 1923, Mr. Eagan left the company's stock in trust for the benefit of his employees. If that is not practicing the Golden Rule, one has to wonder what is.

In contrast to what Mr. Eagan accomplished and what the

company he created has done over the last one hundred years, some of the companies listed in the management book, *In Search of Excellence*, by Tom Peters and Robert Waterman are not so excellent only twenty-three years later. Those companies may have strayed from their core principles or discarded them (having worked for one of the companies, the author knows that it did stray from its core ideology almost to a disastrous effect).

What is distressing is how many excellent companies change so quickly and become something less—sometimes something far less. For example, one of those excellent companies included in Peter's Book, *In Search for Excellence*, entered bankruptcy in 2005. It does appear then, at least in the author's opinion, that consistency and consistent application of the Golden Rule make a difference to those companies searching for excellence and for those wishing to maintain that excellence.

If a company abandons its core ideology, for whatever reason, it is not surprising that the company loses its competitive edge. That conclusion is one lesson that reading *In Search of Excellence* twenty-three years after its writing provides. One does have to speculate about what would have happened to ACIPCO if Mr. Eagan had not left his stock in trust for the company and management had not continued to follow biblical principles—of course, we cannot answer that question because the company *did* hold to its founder's convictions. The question is intriguing, nevertheless.

From that, we can see that effective management goes beyond a one-time effort. Rather, it means a continuous 100 percent effort—not just when you feel like it or after you have read the latest, faddish management book.

The Golden Rule is an imperative. It is not optional. It contains no waivers or carve-outs. It is not subject to modification or rationalization. It does not meet the requirements of moral relativism or secular humanism. It does not conform to any heresy that pretends to care for man but that ultimately results in the perversion and weakening of man's moral structure or foundation. Rather, it is absolute.

FOOTNOTES

[1] *Merriam-Webster's Collegiate Dictionary.* 10th ed, s.v. "love."

[2] See *Vine's Complete Expository Dictionary of Old and New Testament Words* for a more complete discussion.

[3] The author's paraphrase of Matt 22:36.

[4] Remember that the apostle Nathanael when first learning about Jesus from Phillip asked, "What good can come out of Nazareth?" [Author's paraphrase—see John 1:46.]

[5] Matt. 22.37-40 NIV.

[6] The second commandment regarding the proscription of idol worship does not command love of God but only contains a promise that He will show love to those that love Him so long as they abide with His commandments. (See Exodus 20:4 and Deuteronomy 5:8.)

[7] Deut. 6:4-5 NIV. Note that the NAS uses the word "mind" instead of the word "strength."

[8] Lev. 19:18 NIV.

[9] Prov. 1:7, American Bible Society, *The Holy Bible: The Good News Translation.* 2nd ed., (New York: American Bible Society, 1992).

[10] James 1:22-25 NIV.

[11] Rom. 3:23 NIV.

[12] Federer, William J., "Charles Dickens" in *Great Quotations: A Collection of Passages, Phrases, and Quotations Influencing Early and Modern World History Referenced According to Their Sources in Literature, Memoirs, Letters, Governmental Documents, Speeches, Charters, Court Decisions and Constitutions,* (St. Louis, MO: AmeriSearch, 2001).

13 Ps. 8:4 NIV.

14 "For it is by grace you have been saved, through faith—and this not from your-selves, it is the gift of God—not by works, so that no one can boast." Eph. 2:8-9 NIV. [Verse numbers omitted.]

15 Cynics like to point to Christians as hypocrites—much like Jesus called the scribes and Pharisees hypocrites. Being born again generally does mean a change in lifestyle, mores, morals, and standards. Nevertheless, Christians will continue to sin since their human sinful nature will pop out repeatedly. However, true Christians are those who try to do God's work and live the way God wants them to live—they are sinners and sometimes hypocrites, nevertheless, they do try to follow God's will with His and the Holy Spirit's help.

However, not all purported Christians are actually Christians. They may be intel-lectual assenters or they may be joiners. Intellectual assenters accept the philoso-phy. However, they have not made the turn-around inherent in the term "born again." Joiners, on the other hand, are those people who join the Church for a variety of reasons and may not indeed be true Christians—that is, Jesus has not entered their hearts. People sometimes join a church the same way may they join a country club or a social organization such as Kiwanis—many times just for the business or social contacts.

16 *Love Story*. Directed by Arthur Hiller. 16mm, 100 min. Paramount Pictures, Los Angeles, 1970.

17 This is a book about applying the Holy Bible to business, wherever a business is domiciled or located, because such principles provide practical business manage-ment techniques useful for any business—whether domestic or international. Nevertheless, you should note that other religions and cultures espouse what the West calls the Golden Rule.

For example, Buddhism teaches that there is an eight-fold path to enlighten-ment—right view, right intentions, right speech, right action, right livelihood, right effort, right mindfulness, and right concentration. Within right action, Lama Surya Das, points out in his book, *Awakening the Buddha Within*, "Right Action often comes down to the age-old principle: Treat others as you wish to be treated yourself." Lama Surya Das, *Awakening the Buddha Within* (New York: Broadway Books, 1997), 198.

18 Luke 10:25 NIV.

19 Luke 10:29 NIV.

20 Garry Willis in his book, *What Jesus Meant*, points out that he believes that the Levite and the priest avoided the man because he was technically unclean. Based

on that view, the Levite and the priest let their own interpretations of the law, and their concern for minutiae, override God's overreaching principle to love your neighbor as yourself. (Garry Willis, *What Jesus Meant* (New York: Penguin Group, 2006.)

[21] John Hyrcanus was a Hasmonean high priest and ruler of Palestine in the second century BC. His father was Simon, one of the Maccabees—the other two were Judah, who was called truly called Maccabee (or hammerer), and Jonathan. The Maccabees carried on the revolt of their father, Mattathias, against Seleucid Syria. Syria's king, Antiochus Epiphanes, attempted to Hellenize both the Jews and the Jewish religion. As a result, the Maccabean revolt occurred.

[22] Thomas J. Peters and Robert H. Waterman Jr., "Man Waiting for Motivation," in *In Search of Excellence, Lessons from America's Best-Run Companies* (New York: Warner Books, 1982).

[23] Peters and Waterman suggest the use of competition to increase productivity within a company. Such a technique is not generally one that the Golden Rule prescribes but is one that the author has seen work effectively.

Peters and Waterman in their book demonstrate that competition is effective. Again, we encounter a paradox: such competition is good for you and your neighbor, and, although specifically not within the Golden Rule, such competition produces the same results.

[24] Sam Harris, *The End of Faith: Religion, Terror and the Future of Reason* (New York: W. W. Norton & Company, 2005), 186-187.

[25] So eating, at least in the author's home state of Alabama, costs you extra. It does seem strange that some governments tax a necessity of life but that will have to be the subject for another book. Perhaps government could learn from the Golden Rule, but, of course, in the Western world, secular governments make the rules, which they often make without regard to scriptural principles.

[26] Isa. 10:1-3 NIV says:
Woe to those who make unjust laws,
to those who issue oppressive decrees,
to deprive the poor of their rights
and withhold justice from the oppressed of my people,
making widows their prey
and robbing the fatherless.
What will you do on the day of reckoning,
when disaster comes from afar?
To whom will you run for help?
Where will you leave your riches?

27 *Oxford NIV Scofield Study Bible*, Edited by C. I. Scofield, New International Version, (New York: Oxford University Press, 1978), 1235. Scofield, in a reference to a verse in Ephesians, suggests that the word son used in this and other Pauline texts refers not to a gender relationship but to a relationship "of position." Therefore, God puts all believers into the uppermost position in His view because of the Christian's inheritance of that position from Jesus Christ.

Unfortunately, but not unexpectedly, the men who wrote and later translated the Bible, which, when taken as a whole, contains God's absolute truth, were raised within and influenced by their own particular culture and those influences are reflected in their writings. For example, the translation of the King James Bible by eminent Anglican scholars into Elizabethan English for a Scottish, Presbyterian king suffers to some extent from the translator's cultural biases and religious beliefs. The cultural bias and religious belief of the King James interpreters is one reason the King James Version repeatedly uses the word bishop in certain books such as 1 Timothy when referring to the church hierarchy—Anglicans had, and still have, bishops although many other Protestant religions do not.

Here I use the word bias, not in its negative sense as some sort of discrimination, but, rather, in its more neutral sense as meaning the reflection of one's education, culture, and understanding. Of course, a negative bias can reside within those societal factors.

28 Stephen L. Carter, *Integrity* (New York: BasicBooks, 1996), 239.

29 I truly believe that discrimination is sin because it runs counter to God's love for all humanity.

30 John 4:41 NIV.

31 Luke 6:32-36 NIV.

32 American Cast Iron Pipe Company, "History," in *ACIPCO Centennial*, at http://www.acipcocentennial.com/history.html.

CHAPTER 5

CONTRACTS— TERMS AND NEGOTIATIONS

Much of business law deals with contracts and breaches of contracts. A contract consists of an agreement between at least two people, includes promises by each party, requires actions by each party, requires the provision of services or products by one party to another, and requires the other party to compensate the other for the services and products provided, generally via monetary payment.

INTRODUCTION TO CONTRACTS

According to *Black's Law Dictionary*, a contract requires certain essentials, including "competent parties, subject matter, a legal consideration, mutuality of agreement, and mutuality of obligation."[1] Generally, contracts also include such things as time for performance, time of payment, form of payment, indemnifications, remedies, guarantees, and representations and warranties by both parties.

Contracts are also enforceable under the law by specific performance or, depending on the breach, damages against the defaulting party.[2] Stephen L. Carter, a Yale law professor, in his book *Integrity* summarized this latter contractual dictum (originally posited by Justice Oliver Wendell Holmes of the U.S. Supreme Court) as, "the obligation created by a promise is simply the choice to perform a promise or pay damages for its breach."[3]

For example, an agreement between two parties—where one sells an asset and another buys the asset—is called a purchase and sales agreement. General contract law applies to such an agreement—it involves two or more competent parties, consideration, "mutuality of obligation," and "mutuality of agreement."

In the purchase and sales agreement, the parties agree to the purchase price of the asset—the "how much" provision. The parties also agree as to the "how and when." That is, "how and when" the buyer will pay the purchase price, "how and when" the seller will convey the asset, the "how and when" of each parties' promises, etc.

Of course, in some cases, such as sales of real estate, the buyer will want a special conveyance document, such as a deed. Additional documents may include a note, which is itself a form of a contract, security instruments, or a guarantee of performance—for example, a guarantee of a note by a third party or a personal guarantee by the owner in the case of a small company.

Such a sales contract generally follows the rules of common sense and memorializes the intents, rights, duties, and obligations (including those in breach) of the parties to each other with regard to the buying and selling transaction. These provisions deal with the "what of the contract" such as what constitutes breach and what rights and duties of the parties are included. These other provisions also deal with the how—for example, how the wronged party pursues action against the breaching party.

Such a purchase and sales contract is by its nature reciprocal—in other words, what one party gives up, the other party receives. Accordingly, the buyer wishes to increase the number of seller obligations in order to protect himself should the asset received in the transaction prove deficient in some way or, in the alternative, the seller fails to perform one or more of his specific duties.

On the other hand, the seller wants to decrease the number of his duties and obligations to which he is subject. The seller also wishes to limit the time of his various obligations.

The natural friction between the buyer and the seller is what drives the negotiation and contract process. Therefore, the buyer will seek as much protection as he can and the seller will strive to provide less protection. In contractual terms, the buyer will want more express indemnifications, express guarantees, representations, and warranties. On the other hand, the seller will want to provide less of those same things.

BIBLICAL CONTRACTS

The Bible contains very few express prohibitions concerning contracts or their various provisions. It does contain restrictions on interest and lying. It also requires compliance in the areas of fairness and promises (sometimes referred to as vows in the Old Testament). The Old Testament also provides for some interesting redemption provisions applying to the sales of land.

In this latter regard, Leviticus does say that "[i]f you sell land to one of your countrymen or buy any from him, do not take *advantage* of each other"[4] [emphasis added]—in other words, Leviticus espouses the use of the Golden Rule in sales of real estate. In this case, the Lord required fairness in the transaction. Accordingly, at least in a real estate transaction, the Old Testament buyer expected no warnings or disclosures since the Lord required the seller to be fair.

In contrast, in the case of a modern real estate sale, or in the case of any sale for that matter, we warn a buyer to beware of the seller's motives (the term we use is caveat emptor, which comes from Latin and means, "let the buyer beware"). Some express a commonsensical skepticism or cynicism to the seller's motives by colloquially asking, "Why's the other guy selling?"

Since the heart of a contract is a promise, the Old Testament does require that you meet your obligations by not lying (see Lev. 19:11). Not meeting a promise is a lie—a lie to the other person, or persons, to the contract. Further, in the book of Numbers the Lord requires compliance with promises (vows) by saying: "This is what the Lord commands: When a man makes a vow to the Lord or takes an oath to obligate himself by a pledge, he must not break his word but must do everything he said."[5] Contemporarily, in this regard, Carter in *Integrity* states that, "Our respect for contracts, as for other forms of commitment, surely rests on the belief that a person of integrity will do what she has promised, because it is her responsibility to weigh the risk before making the promise."[6]

Of course, the Lord provides the ultimate example of a person keeping his promises. For instance, in Acts 13:32, "We tell you the good news: What God promised our fathers he has fulfilled for us, their children, by raising up Jesus."[7]

The Old Testament also contains some strange provisions regarding the return of property and debts that we would find unworkable in our modern, capitalistic society. As you will remember from previous chapters, God provided the Old Testament to the Jews as a guide to an emerging society and some of those rules, accordingly, do not apply to us.

For example, in Leviticus 25, in the year of the Jubilee, which occurred every fifty years, a buyer returned land to its previous owner. In essence, the buyer had what we call a ground lease (a lease of land for an extended period without actual transfer by deed of the property). In this ground lease, the Lord provided that the seller base the rent on the number of years remaining to the next Jubilee—with more years, obviously, resulting in a higher cumulative rent and, conversely, fewer years a lower cumulative rent. Further, the Lord banned permanent sales of land because He asserted that the land belonged to Him and that the Israelites were solely His tenants. As you can see from this latter explanation, the Lord intended this return provision to apply specifically to Palestine and the Jews living there.

Leviticus also provided for a right of redemption. That is, a poor man's relative could redeem land sold if the poor man could not. The redemption price equaled the original purchase price less the rental applicable to the number of years the buyer (the ground lessor) had used the property. Regardless, in the year of Jubilee, the buyer returned the land to the original owner. However, as with most legal requirements, there was an exception.

That is, God provided certain improved real estate with limited redemption rights. The Law contained only a one-year right of redemption for sales of houses within walled cities, such as Jerusalem. Under this exception, the house became the permanent possession of the buyer if the seller did not redeem the house during the one-year redemption period.[8] Nevertheless, the law considered houses in non-walled cities as unimproved land (pasture). The Lord provided for the return in the year of the Jubilee of the unimproved land.

The law also provided for the forgiveness of debts every seven years (see Deut. 15:1). Later, when the Jews became traders, this provision probably caused some problems. You can probably imagine that under such regimen, most debts contained a balloon payment provision and a maturity just prior to the end of the seven-year period (at least, that is probably how any modern lawyer worth his minimum retainer would structure the transaction).

Further, the Old Testament provided that a creditor could not charge excessive interest (see Deut. 23:19). Similarly, in the Mosaic book of Leviticus, if a fellow Israelite became financially distressed, the Lord prohibited the charging of interest to that person (see Lev. 25:36).[9] However, the non-interest law contained an exception. Interestingly, the Lord allowed an Israelite to charge a foreigner interest (Deut. 23:20) even if it was usurious, or excessive.

The Lord also instructed the Israelites not to sell food at a profit to a financially distressed individual (see Lev. 25:37). Rather, God, through Moses, instructed Israelites to apply the Golden Rule to the financially distressed and said to "help him as you would an alien or a temporary resident, so he can continue to live among you."[10] Note that a supposedly unloving, uncaring, killing, and massacring Old Testament God required that the Israelites display kindness not only to each other but to the an alien or a temporary resident as well for He says to "help him *as you would* an alien or temporary resident...."[11] [Emphasis added.]

CONSIDERATION

Consideration is an essential element of a contract. Without consideration there is no contract (see Restatement Second, Contracts, §§ 17(1), 71).

Essentially, consideration is what each party to the contract gives up—for example, in a car sale, the dealer gives up a car and the buyer gives up money (even if that money is borrowed). Consideration does not necessarily have to consist of money; it can consist of other rights or interests. For example, most contracts start with a phrase such as "for the sum of $100,000 and for other good and valuable consideration, the sufficiency of which is hereby acknowledged, XYZ Corporation conveys to ZYX

Corporation all rights, title, and other interests in such personal property as more particularly described herein." For example, the sale of most assets conveys upon the buyer the unfettered right to sell the asset in the future without any seller restrictions unless the contract specifies such other seller rights (such as the right of first refusal). Similarly, the buyer also may pledge or hypothecate the asset as collateral for a loan without the seller's or anyone else's permission (unless of course, he has already financed the property with a financial institution that may prohibit other financing of the property even with subordinate debt so long as the first financial institution's debt is outstanding).

In an arms-length transaction, consideration presumably amounts to the fair value of the rights, interests, and property conveyed. However, the seller, as owner, knows more about the conveyed property and may value it more, or less, than the purchase price. On the other hand, the buyer may value the property more or less than the seller, depending on a variety of factors the buyer considers as value determinative.

In business, this difference in value perception results in the negotiation of the purchase price. In large transactions, for example, the buyer will probably perform due diligence to ensure he is buying what he thinks he is buying and there are no unknown or hidden problems.

Sometimes, the buyer's due diligence results in an adjustment to the purchase price. Such adjustments often result during a real estate transaction or a business acquisition.

In a real estate purchase, the buyer may find during due diligence that the property requires certain repairs—a reduction in the purchase price equal to the cost of such needed repairs or renovations often results in such situations—however, sometimes the seller may agree to perform the repairs, subject to buyer inspection, prior to sale.

Similarly, in a business acquisition, the buyer may feel that certain assets, such as accounts or notes receivable, are subject to a high probability of non-payment and will want a purchase price reduction for such perceived risk. Or, the buyer may become aware of some liability that he believes justifies a reduction in the purchase price.

Regardless, the lesson here is that those entering contracts should not let the love of money (more about this later) result in one party taking advantage of the other—which is generally the seller, since the seller has a more intimate knowledge of the product, the right, or the interest he is selling.

In other words, taking advantage of another does not result in repeat business, especially when you realize that the seller took advantage of you. As Reichheld and Teal explain in their book, *The Loyalty Effect: The Hidden Force Behind Growth, Profits, and Lasting Value*, the customer is a business constituent deserving loyalty (the others include vendors, stakeholders, and employees). Often, making more profit on one deal or treating the customer unfairly results in the customer not returning.

CONSIDERATION IN CONSUMER DEALINGS

The Golden Rule applies to consideration (where consideration means the price and terms) in consumer dealings as well. In addition, Reichheld's warnings regarding loyalty, as discussed above, apply to consumer transactions.

As an example of how some companies have overlooked the effect of consideration on consumer transactions, look at the deals the phone companies at one time offered new customers. The various long distance phone companies offered new customers checks or lower rates (or the combination of both) to switch their long distance business to them. Unfortunately, although these business practices (buying the business and lowering rates) may temporarily attract a customer, it may prove self-defeating in customer retention. In addition, lowering rates generally has the effect of lowering rates for everyone in the business as Adam M. Brandenburger and Barry J. Nalebuff point out in their book, *Co-opetition*.[12]

Now pretend for a minute that you are the CEO of a long-distance company. You are aware that your competitor from (let us say, a long-distance company headquartered in Mississippi) is providing special deals to new customers, and even offering them checks for changing from your long distance service to theirs. What do you do?

Many of the other long distance companies decide to offer similar deals, although with their own special deals, twists, and marketing approaches. You decide to do so, too, and to match the competition, you also decide to attract new customers with checks for switching—of course, you do not offer your current customers the same deal, for after all, they are already paying a higher rate—why should you lower it? In addition, since they are already customers, there is no need to pay them.

Unfortunately, your customers can see, read, and hear. They receive all the same direct mail advertisements and solicitations—perhaps not from you but from the other phone companies. Your customers, while watching their favorite ball game, hear about a special long-distance, low-price offer from their favorite, allegedly dumb, ex-quarterback (say an ex-quarterback who played pro football where three rivers converge, where it snows heavily, and whose team won a number of Super Bowls) that involves your company.

Consequently, how do you think, say, a loyal customer of twenty years or so feels. Does he feel like he is your neighbor? Does he feel like you are applying the biblical Golden Rule? On the other hand, does he feel that you are applying one of the non-biblical business Golden Rules? The answers, if you are wondering, are no, no, and yes. No, he does not feel like your neighbor. No, he does not feel like you are applying the Golden Rule. Yes, he does feel that you are "doing unto him before he does unto you."

The consequences of these answers could result in a lost customer, especially one who decides that he can apply one of the other non-biblical Golden Rules to you—that is, "don't get mad, get even." Consequently, your customer accepts the offer from the other company, receives a check for switching, and obtains a lower rate (albeit subject to a number of fine print rules and a monthly minimum). In this event, you lose a good, loyal customer who decided to take the special deal and cash the check because you did not acknowledge his loyalty and treat him as fairly as you did an unknown customer from off the street.

Here, your desire (remember you are the long distance company) to maintain billing rates for old customers at the same level results in a double whammy to your earnings. First, you lose the customer and his normal monthly long-distance bill. Second, you now have to spend money to find another customer but, unfortunately, at a lower long distance rate since you have had to meet the competition for new customers by lowering your rates. Third, you have to pay out a check to obtain the new customer since the rest of competition is providing them.

Accordingly, instead of keeping a loyal customer, you lose a customer whom you knew, a customer who had demonstrated loyalty to you, and a customer for whom you had already spent money acquiring and developing.

You probably ask here what you could have done differently. You may have offered lower rates for your existing customers as a reward for their continued business rather than trying to buy the business of new customers. Buying business, as explained above, just resulted in a double whammy impact to the earnings of your company.

In fact, you may have ended up with a triple whammy impact on earnings when you get the same customer back. Of course, you and your competitors taught him churning—that is, you have taught the consumer to take the latest check and the latest lower rate plan and then do it over again the next chance he gets. You really have to wonder about the smarts of some companies (of course, the company from Mississippi ultimately ended up in bankruptcy and an ex-CEO sentenced to twenty-five years in jail).

Now, some companies (you can now stop pretending to be the long distance carrier) may have learned the biblical Golden Rule and understood that the lessons of the Good Book can prove to be good business. Those companies would have realized the importance of keeping the customer even if it means a reduced profit margin. Even a reduced profit margin is better than the alternatives—no profit margin (because a customer left), a negative margin (a least for a while) from those new customers who have accepted a check offer, or a continuing negative margin for those customers who are now churning their accounts.

Alternatively, some companies realize that fairness can result in making a sale, retaining customers, or creating new ones. For example, some of the smarter companies (the author cannot call the others any names because that would subject him to hell fire according to Jesus, see Matthew 5:22, but you get the point) will match prices of a competitor. Of course, to keep the customer honest, the company will require that the customer prove the lower price through such things as a direct mail advertisement or a newspaper clipping.

In this case, a wise company matching the price of a competitor makes a sale it might not have otherwise made. Remember the reason you want customers in the store is so you can sell them something. In addition, the wise company probably creates a loyal customer since the consumer now feels that he will get the best price when shopping at that particular store and, more importantly, he will feel fairly treated. The fairly treated customer will retain that memory much longer than the sales price of the item he bought or the item he purchased that day.

As another example, putting the retention of customers above money (or consideration if you will) also relates to such things as late charges, the reversal of charges (including late charges), or discounts. Here, the wise company allows those who deal directly with the customer to waive or abate certain charges.

Say, for example, a good customer with a history of continuous prompt payment suddenly pays late one month. Now, this customer, knowing that he is a good customer, may call and request a waiver of the late payment because of some exigency that resulted in late payment (e.g., out of town, family emergency, hospitalization, death in the family, natural disaster, etc). In this case, a waiver of the late penalty will probably help retain the customer and demonstrate fairness on your part.

On the other hand, strict enforcement of the consumer's contract, which generally requires a late fee if the customer pays late, may result in "cutting off your nose to spite your face" (pardon the Southern colloquialism). For in this case, the customer knows he is a good customer and expects a little understanding should he inadvertently make a late payment because of some unforeseen circumstance (especially if the payment is just a little late or the amount involved is relatively small).

If the company does not waive the late fee, the consumer may bolt. You just have to wonder whether the company's desire for extra income (its love of money) causes it to do something unwise and unfair. After all, the company incurred a cost to acquire the customer and could ruin a good relationship with just one obtuse act, and lose the customer's business forever. A plethora of other companies awaits the business of this good paying and loyal customer. The unwise company for the extra income derived from one late fee, loses a customer, and now must incur the high costs of obtaining a replacement. Not only that, the customer, according to some statistics, will relate his bad experience to at least twenty-five other people—not exactly good advertising.

This does not mean that you should not regularly enforce contracts. The above discussion just suggests that you apply judgment and common sense when enforcing contractual provisions. Common sense in this view is just wisdom obtained through experience.

Contracts are by nature reciprocal—that is, they are a two-way street. Therefore, the consumer should also treat business fairly even if it costs them to do so, which is the heart of the Golden Rule. Those who regularly abuse the system and the Golden Rule will receive their reward. This will be discussed later as it applies to the story of Lazarus and the rich man.

CONSIDERATION IN BUSINESS DEALINGS

Vendor Dependency

As explained above, Reichheld and Teal describe how to generate loyalty in your business dealings with customers (discussed above), vendors (suppliers), stakeholders, and employees—all of whom help a business succeed. In this regard, a business needs to treat its vendors as fairly as it does its customers. Again, the Golden Rule comes into effect and a business should apply that rule in its business dealing with its vendors. Jesus, in explaining the Golden Rule, does not provide for any exclusions or carve-outs to it.

As an example of a violation of the Golden Rule with respect to dealing with vendors, consider the following hypothetical example. A company may misuse its relationship with a vendor and obtain the lowest possible price from the vendor through coercion. This book calls this coercive technique, for the lack of a better term, vendor dependency.

In this hypothetical situation, a large customer of a manufacturer creates vendor dependency through large purchases of the vendor's goods during a contractually specified term. However, once the vendor has staffed up, expanded its operations to handle increased product shipments, and increased its concentration of business with the large customer, the customer will then, at the end of the contract and during negotiation of the new contract, come in and pressure the manufacturer for a lower price.

In this case, the vendor unhappily reduces the price because it made the mistake of concentrating too much business with one customer. The vendor is now in the unenviable position of having paid for, or borrowed for, new plant and equipment and finds it needs the large customer's business in order to pay for that added plant and equipment. Accordingly, the vendor will lower his price because the alternative may mean financial difficulties for the manufacturer (vendor). This practice by the large customer, in essence, amounts to extortion, but is apparently legal.[13]

Now, many modify the aphorism "all is fair in love and war" by adding "and business" to that phrase—that is, "all is fair in love, war, and business." However, the above described practice is at its best unethical. Although the practice described is extremely slimy, despicable, and underhanded, the government does not legally proscribe it.[14]

Nonetheless, regardless of secular legality, such a practice is not fair and does not correspond to the Golden Rule. It does, however, correspond to one of the twisted Golden Rules described previously—specifically, "do unto others before they do unto you."

In the end, such a vendor dependency practice will prove detrimental to the buyer. Word will spread and the buyer will find that vendors will probably now carefully deal with that buyer and, perhaps, demand contractual terms that prevent the use of such an extortive practice and its consequences to the vendor (the manufacturer in this case). Obviously, such an extortive technique does not provide for vendor loyalty—which Reichheld and Teal feel is one of the keys to business success.

The concentration of business with any one customer does present a company with other business risks—reliance on any one company or industry can increase a business's risks of failure if that primary company or industry has a downturn. For example, in 2005, because of a slowdown in auto sales, automakers negotiated discounts with their vendors.

Although the Bible does not specifically prescribe or recommend business concentration, a wise man or company would avoid such a concentration. As the section on wisdom suggests, wisdom comes from experience and experience teaches men to watch where they tread and what to avoid. Commonsensically, such a concentration of business with one business or industry is unwise. In Proverbs 1:29-33 the Lord warns against such action:

> Since they hated knowledge and did not
> choose to fear the Lord, since they would not
> accept my advice and spurned my rebuke,
> they will eat the fruit of their ways and be
> filled with the fruit of their schemes. For the
> waywardness of the simple will kill them, and
> the complacency of fools will destroy them;
> but whoever listens to me will live in safety
> and be at ease, without fear of harm. [Verse
> numbers omitted.][15]

From a historical perspective, John D. Rockefeller used a similar underhanded trick in his dealing with the railroads that shipped oil to his refineries. In his practice, however, he demanded from the railroads a kickback and information about the shipments of his competitors. Rockefeller obtained such discounts because of the railroad's concentration of business with his company, Standard Oil (which the government later split up because of its monopolistic and anti-trade practices).

Asking the Most from Vendors and Providing the Least in Response

In other cases, a business may request that a vendor or service provider expedite a shipment or service and then complain or refuse to pay for the vendor's extra expediting costs, such as overtime. Of course, you will probably say that the vendor should have protected himself by requiring a purchase order or a contract specifying the terms. However, vendors or service providers, in an effort to meet the needs of a customer, will often begin the process without the necessary paperwork.

Now suppose you were the vendor, do you think the customer applied the rules of scriptural conduct outlined in the Golden Rule or the concept of agápe love with its inherent concept of fairness? Remember that Jesus' definition of "love your neighbor" is an imperative and does not contain any exceptions. In addition, Jesus' definition of neighbor includes everyone, including those you hate (see the story of the Good Samaritan and the Sermon on the Mount). For example, in the Sermon on the Mount Jesus said:

> You have heard that it was said, "Love your neighbor and hate your enemy." But I tell you: Love your enemies and pray for those who persecute you, that you may be sons of your Father in heaven. He causes his sun to rise on the evil and the good, and sends rain

on the righteous and the unrighteous.[16]
[Verse references and footnotes omitted.]

In other cases, the customer will pay the vendor or service provider late—that is, after the vendor has provided what some companies call "exceptional customer service."[17] In some cases, the vendor or service provider may have to bug the customer for payment. Again, is the purchaser following the Golden Rule?

Of course, the object of this book is to teach businessmen how to apply the Golden Rule. However, those who do not believe in the Golden Rule need to prepare for the consequences—more about this later.

FOOTNOTES

[1] Henry Campbell Black, *Black's Law Dictionary*, Abridged 6th ed. (St. Paul, Minn.: West Publishing Co., 1991), s.v. "contract."

[2] The author is not an attorney and the above summarizes the author's general knowledge of contract law strictly as a layman. Accordingly, the legal aspects of contract law are beyond the scope of this book and this book, does not purport to offer legal advice. Anyone involved in contract negotiation, drafting, interpretation, execution, or any other contract matter should contact competent legal counsel.

[3] Carter, p.34.

[4] Lev. 25:14 NIV.

[5] Num. 30:1-2 NIV.

[6] Carter, p. 33.

[7] Acts 13:32-33 NIV. This act fulfilled the Lord's promise to David in the Davidic Covenant.

[8] Interestingly, some states provide for a right of redemption with regard to foreclosed property. Under those redemption laws, the previous owner may redeem his

former property for the payment of the debt and other specified payments, such as accrued interest.

[9] Note the contrast to modern society. At least in the US, we, generally, increase the interest to a so-called default rate of interest.

[10] Lev. 25:35 NIV.

[11] Ibid.

[12] Adam M. Brandenburger and Barry J. Nalebuff, *Co-opetition* (New York: Currency Doubleday, 1996). Note, however, that price fixing is against the law. Brandenburger and Nalebuff just point out the obvious consequences of lowering price to obtain market share.

[13] Price pressures have caused financial difficulties for automotive part suppliers who as a general rule sell only to a limited number of car manufacturers. At the writing of this book, one such supplier had entered bankruptcy and another was restating its financial statements.

[14] Again, the author is not an attorney, cannot provide legal advice, and cannot tell you whether the described practice is "legally" unfair. Whether a practice is unfair depends on the fair trade practices laws governed by state and federal law, particularly the rules and regulations of the Federal Trade Commission that protect businesses as well as consumers.

[15] Prov. 1:29-33 NIV.

[16] Matt. 5:43-46 NIV.

[17] Collins and Porras in *Built to Last*, in documenting the core ideologies of various companies, say that American Express wants to provide "heroic customer service;" Marriott wants to provide "friendly service and excellent value;" Nordstrom wants to provide "service to the customer above all else;" and Wal-Mart wants "to provide value to our customers."

CHAPTER 6

APPLYING THE GOLDEN RULE

Business uses various documents to initiate, convey, and secure business transactions. Most of those documents are contractual in one way or another including notes, mortgages, bills of sale, service contracts, purchase agreements, loan agreements, and purchase orders, among others. Such documents may contain the following provisions:

- the term of the contract
- the price
- a description of the property conveyed or the services provided
- conveyance language or a promise regarding services
- the interest rate for a note
- payment terms
- default provisions
- grace periods
- representations
- limitations
- warranties
- indemnifications
- the specified collateral
- collateral release provisions

- documents required prior to closing the transaction, if any
- fees
- late charges
- guarantees
- the amount loaned in a note
- required disclosures in a continuing relationship (such as the quarterly or annual provision of financial statements)
- revolving features of a loan
- hold harmless covenants
- default provisions
- other covenants (such as required debt-to-equity ratios for business loans)

CONSUMER CONTRACTS

Generally, the most negotiation in a consumer sales transaction involves price. The consumer often finds that the only thing he can negotiate is price and he can often only do so by using his feet—that is, by leaving and going to another store with a lower price.

However, the consumer in larger transactions does have some price negotiation ability such as in home or car purchases. On the other hand, many of the terms a consumer can obtain in a consumer borrowing or leasing transaction do not involve negotiation but, rather, choice. For example, the consumer in a lending transaction may choose the amount of the loan, the term of the loan, a loan's balloon provisions, a loan's amortization requirements (whether 30 or 15 years, etc.), the payment amount (which may vary if the loan involves any interest only or variable payment features), and loan amount (which may increase in loans with negative amortization).[1]

The other terms of a consumer transaction, however, are

generally non-negotiable because the consumer often has no bargaining power. To the business, most consumer transactions are not large enough to warrant any negotiation with the consumer—other than the consumer choices previously described. In this regard, most consumer transactions are "take it or leave it" propositions—the consumer either signs standard and pre-prepared documents (left blank for consumer variables such as name and the items of consumer choice mentioned above) or he walks away.

Business generally uses non-negotiable consumer documents. These documents are generally "fill-in the blank" forms providing fill-in spaces for consumer information and variables. Such consumer documents may accommodate consumer choice with addendums, riders, or other specialized documents but such addendums, riders, etc. are also standard except as to the variables of the transaction.

In the use of standard documents, the business wants to ensure that the contract:

- outlines the terms of the transaction and includes all the applicable requirements (such as term, price, interest rate, default interest rate, payment dates, etc.)
- provides the business an appropriate security interest (a perfected security interest for personal property or a mortgage, or deed of trust, for real property)
- ensures adequate compensation in the event of late payment
- complies with all local, state, and federal regulations
- conforms with all contractual aspects to ensure the contract's enforceability

- contains appropriate and legal default provisions
- ensures the consumer's legal capacity to execute the contract
- limits the company's litigation risk (for example, by the use of mandatory arbitration clauses)

These documents are all not as one-sided as they might on the surface appear since federal and state consumer protection laws and the unfair and deceptive practices acts (referred to by some as UDAP) protect the consumer and the standard documents include those protections. The consumer protection laws provide the consumer certain rights including such things as:

- rights of redemption in foreclosure
- rights of rescission in certain transactions
- advanced disclosure of consumer costs in real estate finance transactions
- fair lending
- fair advertising
- fair business practices
- equal credit opportunity
- restriction on the use of credit information (including opt-out provisions)
- consumer privacy
- disclosure of the actual cost of lending, including the provision of the annual percentage rate
- securities brokerage statement requirements
- securities trade confirmation requirements

- provision of a prospectus in a mutual fund transaction
- anti-red lining
- community reinvestment
- anti-churning (also known as flipping or twisting in certain contexts)

Non-compliance with the consumer protection acts may a) allow rescission of a contract at a later date, b) provide for business fines, or c) provide for civil or criminal penalties, depending on Congress's or a legislature's view towards the illegality of a particular business act or omission.

Contract law also protects the consumer, although businesses generally construct a contract in a way that it protects themselves. However, the law of contracts protects the consumer if in the execution of a contract the business commits fraud; this fraud protection applies no matter how valid or enforceable the contract on its surface otherwise is. Further, the wronged party entering into any contract under duress may find the contract void or voidable, depending on the type of duress applied or used—and, in the voidable case, voiding is at the victim's option.

Since most consumers understand that the real meat of a contract relates to default, which at the inception of the contract the consumer does not believe will happen, the consumer may view the contract as mere paperwork without force and effect because default, at least in the consumer's opinion, will not occur. Accordingly, the consumer, under the conviction of such belief, does not read such paperwork because he does not believe his risk warrants such a reading.

Further, even in the absence of this fallacious belief in fate or probabilities, the consumer may reject even reading a contract or note, since the consumer generally only pays attention to the price, the interest rate, the term, and, most importantly in a deferred payment or lending transaction, the payment amount. Regardless, even with the many protections afforded consumers under the various consumer protection and UDAP acts, the business contract with the consumer is generally one-sided to the extent that the business can make it that way without violating some law or making the contract unconscionable.

In view of the realities of the above, the reader should understand that as a businessman, he is still subject to the laws of the Good Book. God's laws usurp, nullify, and supplant any law made by man—no matter how fair or worthy.

Also, as a reminder, the Lord shows in his love a great concern for those who, for whatever reason, cannot protect or negotiate for themselves. To review some of the Lord's concern, please review the following list (some of which the book has previously discussed).

> Do not steal. Do not lie. Do not deceive one another.[2]

> Do not defraud your neighbor or rob him.[3]

> Do not pervert justice; do not show partiality to the poor or favoritism to the great, but judge your neighbor fairly.[4]

> If one of your countrymen becomes poor and is unable to support himself among you, help him as you would an alien or a temporary resident, so he can continue to live among you.[5]

> If there is a poor man among your brothers in any of the towns of the land that the Lord your God is giving you, do not be hardhearted or tightfisted toward your poor

brother. Rather be openhanded and freely lend him whatever he needs. Be careful not to harbor this wicked thought: "The seventh year, the year for canceling debts, is near," so that you do not show ill will toward your needy brother and give him nothing. He may then appeal to the Lord against you, and you will be found guilty of sin. Give generously to him and do so without a grudging heart; then because of this the Lord your God will bless you in all your work and in everything you put your hand to. There will always be poor people in the land. Therefore I command you to be openhanded toward your brothers and toward the poor and needy in your land.[6]

Do not take advantage of a hired man who is poor and needy, whether he is a brother Israelite or an alien living in one of your towns.[7]

Will evildoers never learn—
    those who devour my people as men eat
      bread
    and who do not call on the Lord?
There they are, overwhelmed with dread,
    for God is present in the company of the
      righteous.
You evildoers frustrate the plans of the poor,
    but the Lord is their refuge.[8]

He who oppresses the poor shows contempt
    for their Maker,
    but whoever is kind to the needy honors
    God.[9]

Rich and poor have this in common:
The Lord is the Maker of them all.[10]

Do not exploit the poor because they are
   poor
  and do not crush the needy in court,
for the Lord will take up their case
  and will plunder those who plunder
   them.[11]

Woe to those who make unjust laws,
  to those who issue oppressive decrees,
  to deprive the poor of their rights
  and withhold justice from the oppressed
   of my people,
  making widows their prey
  and robbing the fatherless.[12]

Her prophets whitewash these deeds for them
by false visions and lying divinations. They
say, "This is what the Sovereign Lord says"—
when the Lord has not spoken. The people of
the land practice extortion and commit
robbery; they oppress the poor and needy and
mistreat the alien, denying them justice.[13]

For I know how many are your offenses
  and how great your sins.
You oppress the righteous and take bribes
  and you deprive the poor of justice in the
   courts.
Therefore the prudent man keeps quiet in
   such times,
  for the times are evil.
Seek good, not evil,

that you may live.
Then the Lord God Almighty will be with
    you,
    just as you say he is.
Hate evil, love good;
    maintain justice in the courts.
Perhaps the Lord God Almighty will have
    mercy
    on the remnant of Joseph.[14]

I am not commanding you, but I want to test
the sincerity of your love by comparing it
with the earnestness of others. For you know
the grace of our Lord Jesus Christ, that
though he was rich, yet for your sakes he
became poor, so that you through his poverty
might become rich.[15]

These are the words of the Amen, the
faithful and true witness, the ruler of God's
creation. I know your deeds, that you are
neither cold nor hot. I wish you were either
one or the other! So, because you are
lukewarm—neither hot nor cold—I am about
to spit you out of my mouth. You say, "I am
rich; I have acquired wealth and do not need
a thing." But you do not realize that you are
wretched, pitiful, poor, blind and naked. I
counsel you to buy from me gold refined in
the fire, so you can become rich; and white
clothes to wear, so you can cover your
shameful nakedness; and salve to put on your
eyes, so you can see.[16]

CONSUMER LOANS

As mentioned previously, consumers do not generally negotiate the provisions of a consumer loan. For various reasons, businesses standardize consumer contracts. One reason specifically applicable to a mortgage loan, which was not previously mentioned, is the requirements of the secondary mortgage markets.

The secondary mortgage market is one of the great inventions of the American mortgage system—FHA through the Government National Mortgage Association (Ginnie Mae) started securitization with the introduction of the Ginnie Mae Modified Pass-Through program in the early seventies. The secondary mortgage market cannot operate without document standardization because the market requires the homogeneity of the notes and mortgages contained in and supporting a securitization. In other words, those securitizing mortgages must use standard documents in their securitizations because the market must know legally, without exception, what it is buying.

Although this securitization process ultimately benefits consumers, the process consequentially prevents the consumer from changing most of the documents used in closing a mortgage loan. However, the consumer has wide latitude of choice in the mortgage lending arena—choice that expands almost monthly.

Nevertheless, the fairness concept inherent in the Golden Rule and God's inclusionary rules (which we addressed in the book's discussion of God's anti-discrimination rules) requires that a company provide even-handed documentation, policies, and procedures regarding consumer loans. Of course, this fairness and non-discrimination is often, in consumer transactions, required by law.

Regardless, although the consumer protection laws provide various protections to consumers, lenders, in the opinion of the author, should go beyond just complying with the letter of the law, and should comply with its spirit and go beyond it in the sense of fair play. God's Holy Scripture countenances both.

For example, in the mortgage lending area, the state and the federal government by law and regulation require that mortgage bankers and financial institutions provide a number of disclosure documents to a consumer either at application or at closing. However, no law[17] generally mandates providing the consumer all of the legal closing documents prior to closing—in the same vein, there is no law that prevents a lender from providing those documents either.

In the interest of full disclosure and fair play, it would seem that a lender would desire the borrower to have a fuller understanding of the mortgage process. A lender could facilitate consumer understanding of the documents if the lender provided a plain English translation of the documents[18]—sort of a Mortgage Documents 101, which would include an easily understandable glossary and appendix explaining the meaning of the plethora of acronyms used in the mortgage lending business (or any lending business for that matter).

Alternatively, the lender could use a videotape or DVD to explain the entire process. The lender could require the borrower to view the videotape or DVD at application or if the application was taken on-line or by telephone—the lender could send the borrower the videotape or DVD.

In regards to the suggestions above, the lender could also explain prior to closing, in whatever media seem appropriate, information regarding the mortgage note as follows:

1. the borrower's right to repay
2. where the consumer is to pay
3. what the late charges are and when the lender imposes them
4. when default occurs (it occurs upon the

non-payment of a required monthly
payment)
5. joint and several liability (in other words,
each signer and guarantor is responsible
for repayment)
6. prepayment penalties, if any
7. due-on-sale clauses (whether or not the
loan is assumable or not)

In the case of the mortgage or deed of trust (the document
conveying the lender's lien, or security, rights), the lender
could explain in such educational material such things as:

1. the payment application hierarchy (e.g.,
interest, principal, escrow items, late
charges, etc.)
2. the effect of mechanic's liens to the
borrower (new construction)
3. responsibility for payment of insurance
and taxes
4. the consumer's primary obligation
regarding the inspection of the home
5. the lender's liability regarding pre-closing
inspections (in other words, the
inspection is done for the benefit of the
lender and not the borrower)
6. the lack of a guarantee of merchantability
or fitness of the property by the lender
7. what to do if the house is damaged by fire
or other natural causes
8. standard insurance mortgage clauses
9. the lender's rights to hold insurance
proceeds during a restoration period
10. the lender's inspection rights during
restoration

11. the borrower's obligation to maintain the
mortgaged property in good repair
12. the lender's post-closing inspection rights
13. the consequences of default because of
misrepresentation
14. the consequences of monetary default,
including notices, and acceleration
15. the borrower's environmental storage and
usage obligations
16. the borrower's environmental notification
requirements

Under the Real Estate Settlement Procedures Act
(RESPA), a transfer of servicing disclosure is generally
required at closing. Regardless, the lender should explain
what the transfer of servicing entails since it is an often-
misunderstood practice. The lender should explain that it is a
standard practice of the industry, does not affect the
borrower's rights, and will have no consequence on the
servicing of his loan.

These two suggestions, providing the documents and
providing the explanations, would allow the lender to teach
his "neighbor," the consumer, about the mortgage lending
process. The first suggestion would allow the consumer to
understand, read, and obtain counsel regarding the documents
before closing. Reading the documents at closing often
amounts to superficial explanations by a closing agent and
vapid responses from the consumer—after all, once at the
closing table, especially when the deal involves the purchase
of a home or the refinancing of a construction loan, it is too
late for the consumer to back out. Besides, a closing is not a
good place for reading or understanding complicated
documents.

Further, since the closing attorney generally shoves a form
before the borrower that says that the consumer has read and

understands the documents he has signed, it would seem that the honest lender would want the borrower to have actually read and understood the documents. In the alternative, it might appear that the lender at best, had something to hide, or at worst, was committing some sort of mortgage fraud.

Beyond the Consumer Protection Disclosures

RESPA requires that within three days of application, the lender must provide the borrower a good faith estimate (GFE) of settlement costs and a Department of Housing and Urban Development (HUD) prepared booklet relating to settlement costs. A new GFE is required if the consumer chooses another type of loan because the costs of that loan may differ— primarily in regards to points charged.

Regardless, it is still surprising that many lenders do not "hit" the GFE estimates even though they should know the costs of closing a mortgage loan in particular mortgage markets and may even provide the closing agent with closing instructions regarding the amount of the fees, costs, and points the closing agent is to collect at closing. It would seem from a standard of fairness that the consumer should know the cost of the transaction, within tolerances, at the outset of the loan.

However, when HUD suggested such a change to the RESPA regulations in 2002—that is, guaranteed closing costs within tolerances—the industry went apoplectic presumably because they did not like the tight tolerances that HUD provided. Interestingly, the mortgage industry's reaction to the proposed changes ended in HUD withdrawing its proposed regulations in 2004. Regardless, to put the shoe on the other foot, one has to wonder whether mortgage bankers would like to purchase something and not know the final cost until the vendor delivered the item to the lender and it was too late for the lender to back out of the transaction.

Here the Golden Rule and a little common sense could provide a win-win situation for the consumer and the lender.

Again, there is no rule that a mortgage lender not guarantee the cost of closing—and those that offer no cost closings are essentially guaranteeing the cost to themselves anyway. This would seem, at least to the author, a good way to engender borrower loyalty, especially in a business where loan turnover has increased. A surprise at the closing table is not something the borrower is soon to forget and will not probably induce his return to the lender providing such inadequate customer service. Moreover, again as mentioned before, the negative advertising from a surprise closing cost overrun will extend to at least twenty-five of the consumer's acquaintances (and who knows how far it goes from them).

Of course, in the above situation, it is not unreasonable for the lender to provide himself some tolerance for items that might change (for example, the number of required inspections in connection with new construction may vary). Nevertheless, it would seem that the lender could provide a tolerance for such costs or at least a guaranteed maximum.

RESPA, besides the settlement cost booklet and the good faith estimate, requires the use of the HUD-1 as the settlement statement in residential lending transactions. The HUD-1 is now full of so-called junk fees, which lenders and settlement service providers (closing agents, title companies, etc.) use to increase their fees from closing. Such junk fees include a multitude of items, including things such as:

- drop off fees (in New York City)
- courier costs
- faxing costs
- overnight mailing costs
- loan processing fees
- payoff fees
- wire transfer fees
- document preparation fees
- notary fees

- lender underwriting review fees
- lender appraisal review fees
- title search fee
- loan funding fees
- lender application fees
- copying charges
- amortization schedule fees
- warehousing fees
- shipping fee
- what other fee the lender or settlement provider can justify as related to the transaction

Of course, the consumer must understand that the lender and the settlement provider *do not serve* as the consumer's agent. They provide a duty of care only to those they serve and the lender in a secondary market transaction generally looks to the investor as his ultimate customer. In the same way, settlement providers look to the lender as their primary customer—after all, that is where all the repeat business comes from.

Nevertheless, some lenders now understand that junking up an HUD-1 is not a good way to engender repeat business or customer loyalty. This is especially the case if the use of junk fees results in high costs to the consumer.

Many integrated financial institutions view the borrower as potential customer in a variety of areas whether in consumer loans, home equity lines of credit (HELOCs), credit cards, trust services, private banking relationships, self-employed pension plans, car loans, deposit relationships, and broker/dealer services. Accordingly, wise financial institutional leadership will realize that benefiting their neighbor through fair lending fees, no matter the transaction, will engender loyalty, repeat business, and use of the institution's other products and services. A classic win-win situation, as described by Covey, results. In other words, fewer fees on one transaction can mean more financial institution profitability in the end.

One bank does offer such a service. This bank is Dutch but does a great deal of business in the United States. ABN AMRO Mortgage offers its so-called OneFee[SM] loan, which includes a guaranteed aggregate fee, for the following (according to ABN AMRO Mortgage):

- origination fees
- discount points
- appraisal fee
- lender's title insurance and related title services
- lender attorney fee (if required)
- survey (if required)
- flood certification
- credit reports
- tax service fees
- underwriting and processing fees
- recording fees

Certain variable costs of closing, such as prepaid interest that varies depending on when the loan actually closes, are not included. In addition, escrow items for real estate taxes and insurance are not included since they are the responsibility of the borrower (the borrower would likely incur these costs regardless of whether the home has a mortgage or not), and these costs vary depending upon the location of the home and its value. Mortgage insurance is also variable because its costs depend on the amount financed and is the borrower's responsibility—after all, the borrower could have otherwise waited until he had a higher down payment before purchasing a home. In that latter case, he would have avoided mortgage insurance in its entirety if the loan-to-value ratio (the amount of the loan divided by its value) was equal to or less than 80 percent. Finally, OneFee[SM] does not include transfer taxes, intangible taxes, mortgage taxes, and the like, which vary depending on state, county, and local law and the amount financed and sometimes even on the number of pages recorded.

The conclusions of this book and the author's research suggest that ABN AMRO has created a classic win-win situation through the OneFee[SM]. ABN AMRO's reasons for doing this are unknown to the author. Nevertheless, the result is a love your neighbor result—note that love your neighbor does not mean not making a profit but simply means treating your neighbor fairly. In the colloquialism of today, it also means not "ripping your neighbor off."

Interestingly, HUD proposed a one-fee solution in its proposed 2002 RESPA rules changes but the smaller lenders created an uproar because they thought they could not compete in a market where they could not charge all the various junk fees and that a one fee charge gave the larger lenders an unfair advantage. However, it looks like the competition of the free market will often create fairness even when some in the market object to such fairness. Paul's warning to Timothy is particularly appropriate here:

> Command those who are rich in this present world not to be arrogant nor to put their hope in wealth, which is so uncertain, but to put their hope in God, who richly provides us with everything for our enjoyment.
> Command them to do good, to be rich in good deeds, and to be generous and willing to share. In this way they will lay up treasure for themselves as a firm foundation for the coming age, so that they may take hold of the life that is truly life.[19]

In a "welcome letter," the lender tells the borrower where to pay. In addition, in this "welcome letter" the lender offers the borrower the option of making his payments automatically. However, the lender could serve both his and the borrower's needs as well if the welcome letter also addressed what the borrower should do if he encounters financial difficulty—such as a lost job, a natural disaster (such as a hurricane), a call up to military service, or the death of a co-borrower. The borrower should know that apprising the lender of financial difficulties immediately provides him benefits. For example, early notification may allow the lender to help the borrower through forbearance or payment plans while the borrower remedies his financial situation. Early notification also allows the lender to counsel the borrower on his financial situation and to advise the borrower of the various alternatives to foreclosure if, ultimately, the borrower cannot repay. In the twenty-first century, most owners of mortgage notes would prefer remedial action to foreclosure.

Such action will receive God's reward, for as Solomon says in Proverbs, "He who is kind to the poor lends to the Lord, and he will reward him for what he has done."[20] Besides the altruistic reward, a lender's concern for fairness and his display of care towards the borrower on the front-end should again create a win-win situation and customer appreciation and loyalty.

Although most other business transactions are not as complicated as a mortgage lending transaction, the above principles should apply to any business that wants to follow the Good Book's principles. Again, full, understandable, and complete disclosure may prevent collection problems, mitigate damage to the loan's collateral, and reduce the chances of lawsuit. Such disclosure will produce its business rewards today and its spiritual rewards later (but, in relative terms, not so very much later).

THE GOOD, THE BAD, AND THE UGLY

As an example of what *not* practicing the godly principles include, one only need look at so-called predatory lending. Predatory lending simply means that certain bad lenders prey on the poor, the uninformed, the uneducated, and the elderly, to the disadvantage of those groups of people. Remember that the Lord in Leviticus 25:35 says: "If one of your countrymen becomes poor and is unable to support himself among you, help him as you would an alien or a temporary resident, so he can continue to live among you."[21] As you will notice, the Lord's command does not say to take advantage of the disadvantaged. However, in fairness, predatory lending consists of practices conducted by a relatively small minority of the mortgage industry.

For example, the lending practices found within predatory lending include such things as:

- very high fees
- the financing of single-premium credit life within the loan
- balloon loans with short terms
- high interest rates
- negative amortization
- prepayment penalties
- loan churning (referred to as loan flipping)

These abuses have generally occurred in what mortgage lenders call the sub-prime market. The impact of high fees, often up to 8 percent or more, increases the amount the borrower has to repay since the fee is included in the loan amount—in contrast, the normal fees associated with a prime loan aggregate approximately 1.00 percent.[22]

The California Association of Mortgage Brokers, in an

attempt to define predatory lending, issued the following statement at its annual convention. "Predatory lending is defined as intentionally placing consumers in loan products with significantly worse terms and/or higher costs than loans offered to similarly qualified consumers in the region for the primary purpose of enriching the originator and with little or no regard for the costs to the consumer." In other words in most cases predatory lending amounts to fraud (or close to it). The Lord said this regarding fraud:

> Food gained by fraud tastes sweet to a man,
> but he ends up with a mouth full of gravel.
> [Verse number omitted]. 23

Many of the costs incurred by the consumer in a predatory lending case benefit the lender rather than the consumer. For example, single-premium credit life policies provide benefits primarily to the predatory lender rather than to the borrower—such insurance only lasts over the term of the loan, provides no cash value to the borrower, and creates insurance commissions for the predatory lender. The borrower generally finances the lump sum payment for such policies (the single-premium), which increases the loan amount and the borrower's payments.

The lending industry considers any loan with a lump sum payment due at the end of the note's term a balloon loan. Such a practice is not per se predatory since the prime market uses such loans, as does the commercial real estate market. However, the mortgage industry, the federal government, and many states often consider such balloon terms predatory when used in a consumer transaction and when the balloon payment occurs rather quickly, such as after only five years (see the HOEPA restriction explained below).

The effects that high interest rates have on borrowers are self-explanatory. However, the impact is even more harmful when you consider those paying the highest rates are those least able to pay them.

Negative amortization just means the payment is not high enough to pay the interest due. Accordingly, the lender adds the unpaid interest to the principal balance of the loan, which again just makes it harder to pay the loan off because the borrower must make higher payments in the future to pay off the loan over its life.

Prepayment penalties make sure that the loan stays in effect for some period. In other words, the lender wants the loan to remain outstanding for a specified period so that they can receive the high interest rates the predatory loans generally carry. In essence, this practice often prevents the borrower from refinancing when interest rates change because the borrower will have to pay a percentage of the existing loan to refinance (generally, the prepayment penalty starts at 5 percent and goes down 1 percent each year until it is no longer applicable). In contrast, the borrower with a prime loan can generally refinance without penalty.

Loan churning (referred to as loan flipping) means the lender keeps turning the loan over to earn additional fees. Such churning generally provides the borrower with no benefit. The flipping lender, of course, receives fees all over again.

Congress passed HOEPA (the Home Ownership Equity Protection Act) in 1994 to deal with abuses in the sub-prime arena. However, HOEPA has a very limited scope. For example, it applies solely to a refinancing or a closed-end home equity loan and not loans for the construction or purchase of a home.

A significant fault of the legislation is that it deals with so-called high cost loans more through disclosure than through the prohibition of predatory practices, fines, or incarceration for those practicing predatory lending. Actually,

HOEPA does not contain a provision regarding any criminal penalties for failing to follow its provisions.

In addition, as mentioned above, HOEPA does not prohibit such high cost loans but requires expanded disclosures under TILA (the Truth in Lending Act). It does provide, however, the following limitations or prohibitions:

- It limits prepayment penalties for those borrowers who use 50 percent of their gross income to make loan payments;
- It restricts balloon payments for loans with terms of five years or less; and
- HOEPA proscribes negative amortization (that is, the increase in loan balance resulting from payments insufficient to amortize the balance).

Because of the limited federal authority discussed above under HOEPA, the states, and even cities, decided to get involved once they found that predatory lending practices were occurring within their jurisdictions. Accordingly, state, county, and local authorities have placed an increasing emphasis on predatory lending rules.

The state of North Carolina was the first to get into the act and issued the first state legislation addressing predatory lending, which almost became the model act for other states to follow. This act generally applies to high cost loans, which the state defines as loans with fees exceeding 5 percent of the loan balance or loans where the interest rate is more than 8 percent higher than the interest rate on a comparable treasury security. Among other things, the North Carolina anti-predatory lending act prohibits a) the financing of fees, b) balloon payments, c) negative amortization, d) lending where the borrower receives no tangible benefit (this is the anti-flipping provision), and e) does not allow borrowers to finance the cost of single-premium credit life policies inside the mortgage loan. In addition, the act prohibits prepayment penalties for loans of less than $150,000.

Research on the effects of the North Carolina anti-predatory lending act to sub-prime lending within the state has been mixed. Some researchers believe that this act has had no effect on North Carolina sub-prime lending while others, in the alternative, believe that the law has reduced the amount of sub-prime lending in North Carolina. Regardless of this disagreement over the empirical effects, a number of other states and cities have followed North Carolina's lead—making the number of jurisdictions with such laws almost thirty at the writing of this book.

The various anti-predatory lending acts have attracted the attention of lenders, and concerned Wall Street, particularly when some states included assignee liability within their anti-predatory lending acts. Assignee liability means the liability associated with nefarious predatory lending practices would carry over to the purchaser of the mortgage loan—the assignee. However, most states, such as Georgia, generally revised their anti-predatory lending laws when the secondary mortgage market stopped buying high cost loans originated in a state with assignee liability.

At this point, you may wonder why the book has gone into such detail about predatory lending? What is the point of including a description of predatory lending in a book concerning the Good Book and good business? The point is that a group of amoral lenders for the love of money has ripped-off and continues to rip-off the disadvantaged while the rest of the lending industry has stood by and watched.

If the rest of the mortgage industry had stood up and called for action, perhaps there would not be almost thirty statutes covering predatory lending in various states, counties, and cities—a difficult compliance task for a nationwide or even regional mortgage lender. And, perhaps, if the mortgage industry had told Congress that we needed action to stop such practices, or had asked their state legislatures to enact state licensing laws and/or strict codes of enforceable lender ethics, predatory lending may have died, lost its malignancy, or gone into remission.

The Good Book does not call for a reactionary love of your neighbor ex post facto but, rather, proactively. That is, acts of love and fairness should happen before egregious acts occur, if possible. Accordingly, to some extent, love of your neighbor should involve performing acts of love or fairness before harm befalls your neighbor. For example, giving to a benevolent trust as a member of a professional society or organization to provide funds to an unfortunate associate qualifies as such proactive love of your neighbor.

In the alternative, as described above, sometimes loving your neighbor means taking a poisonous snake by its head and breaking its neck. In other words, predatory lending (a snake, in the author's opinion) is not good business and it does not comply with the Good Book's requirements, and needs its neck broken. Of course, as mentioned before, those engaging in bad business practices will receive their reward (if not in this world, then the next)—as a reminder "...thieves nor the greedy nor drunkards nor slanderers nor swindlers will inherit the kingdom of God."[24]

CONSUMER PROTECTION

Laws and Regulations

Many of the laws protecting consumers and investors have come about because of past irresponsible behavior by businesses. Unfortunately, this behavior must become extreme before it comes to the attention of the legislature or Congress. We know that in consumer protection the federal government and the state legislatures generally operate in a reactionary mode. That is, they react to an abuse rather than anticipate abuses in a proactive or preventive matter, and then they only react when a crisis of confidence, a depression, or something similarly harmful or disastrous occurs.

For example, many of the securities laws of this country came about after the stock market crash of 1929. This crash revealed many defects a) in the securities' markets, b) the government's lack of effective regulation, and c) the misbehavior of some dealing in those markets. The Roosevelt Administration proposed and Congress enacted The Securities Act of 1933, The Securities Exchange Act of 1934, The Trust Indenture Act of 1939, The Investment Advisors Act of 1940, and The Investment Company Act of 1940, all in response to the market failures of the early twentieth century. Many of the provisions in those securities acts provide protection for the individual investor, the consumer.

Even before the stock market failure of 1929, some industrial tycoons (such as Rockefeller with Standard Oil) had so monopolized their respective industries and consequently acted so badly and with so little interest in the welfare of the consumer that Congress had to pass acts preventing certain monopolies and monopolistic practices. However, the federal government and the states allowed certain monopolies, such as the public utilities, to continue to exist until some deregulation occurred through the breakup of AT&T into the Baby Bells in 1984, and other deregulation of the energy and telecommunication markets that began to occur in the last twenty years of the twentieth century.

Congress first addressed monopolies in the Sherman Antitrust Act in 1890 and then amended it in 1914 with the Clayton Act because of loopholes contained in the Sherman Antitrust Act. Although not thought of as strict consumer protection statutes, both acts helped the consumer by restricting monopolistic practices, both under the Sherman Antitrust Act and the Clayton Act, and by limiting unfair trade practices in the Clayton Act (as further amended by the Robinson-Patman Act of 1936 and the Celler–Kefauver Act in 1950).

Similarly, the US Congress passed the RESPA in response to the abuses in the real estate settlement area including kickbacks to realtors from lenders—RESPA outlawed such kickbacks and provided for use of HUD-1 at closing, the provision of a GFE, and the settlement cost booklet previously described in this chapter. RESPA under the last two provisions, according to HUD, helped "consumers become better shoppers for settlement services."[25]

Congress enacted the Truth-in-Lending Act in 1968 in order to disclose the actual cost of credit to borrowers in the form of an annual percentage rate, the amount financed, and the total of all payments. Further, Congress passed The Fair Housing Act (1968) and the Equal Credit Opportunity Act (1976) in response to discrimination that was occurring in the lending markets, which those laws now proscribe.

From a layman's perspective and Christian perspective, it appears that business may have prevented most of that consumer protection legislation if business had just treated the consumer fairly and without discrimination, and had policed those in their industry who discriminated or treated people unfairly. Again, the various industries failed to police themselves, as is the case with predatory lending.

Similarly, various industries could have lobbied government to enact legislation that would have required licensing, enforceable codes of ethics, and appropriate sanctions and penalties. Industry could have proposed such legislation, proscribing unfair and discriminatory business practices, before government created its own legislation. In the opinion of the author, legislation enacted with good, objective input from industry and the consumer groups would have resulted in less burdensome, costly, and complex legislation than that ultimately created by government.

However, the ancient Greeks said that nature abhors a vacuum and government abhors a regulatory vacuum even more. Therefore, in the absence of proposed legislation from anyone else, government will create its own legislation, which is often mangled, too full of disclosure, overly complex, and difficult to enforce. One only has to read the annual percentage rate regulations (the U.S. Federal Reserve Board's Regulation Z) to see how complex government can create regulations—regulations that only Ph.D.s can understand.

If good businessmen had stood up for the consumer and had cooperated with government and weeded out the bad businesses and the bad people, then business would not find itself burdened with a ridiculous amount of paperwork, disclosures, and costs. Unfortunately, we now have so many disclosures in certain consumer transactions, such as in lending and securities brokerage, that disclosure has turned into a monster with more heads than the Greek mythological being Hydra (who grew new heads if one was decapitated— sort of like the governmental bureaucracies do). Most consumers do not read, understand, or have the time to read all the forms, reports, and notices that government has forced business to give or send out to the consumer in the name of disclosure in a transaction. What's more, the consumer has no power to negotiate, since business has made most contracts or transactions a "take it or leave it" proposition. Consequently, the consumer just ignores all the paperwork unless the consumer comes to believe that business has harmed them in some way.

Lawsuits

Once a consumer believes business has harmed him, then the consumer will hire an attorney to comb the documents for fault and then sue the offending business for some error or omission or fault in consumer protection compliance. Of course, the plaintiff's bar will attempt to find a pattern of egregious behavior so that they can have a class of harmed individuals certified and a class action commenced.

Sometimes the fault or omission is one that is, or was, inadvertent. However, an error or omission still often results in a lawsuit because of the way Congress and the legislatures have constructed some of these complex, consumer protection laws. For example, many of the consumer protection laws provide a very low threshold for mistakes, inadvertent or otherwise.

Regardless, business may have prevented these lawsuits if they only had used a proactive, Christian doctrine of fairness in their dealings with their neighbors.

Nevertheless, lawsuits do occur. Some of the actions brought as class actions are ridiculous since the lawsuits often only enrich the plaintiff attorney—the consumer in many cases receives de minimis or inconsequential compensation. For example, in the escrow overage cases the individual consumer often receives a few dollars in damages as compared to the millions awarded to the plaintiff law firm.

Criminal Suits

On the other hand, the SEC, FTC, and the attorneys general of the various states (particularly, Attorney General Spitzer of the state of New York), have brought many very justified actions against those who have engaged in unlawful business practices, particularly securities and insurance violations, including fraud—that in some cases harmed not just ordinary consumers but businesses as well.

Spitzer's inquiries have included broker/dealers as large as Merrill Lynch, mutual funds, and insurance advisors such as Marsh & McLennan and have revealed some very serious deceitful and deceptive practices. For example, the lack of independence between Merrill Lynch's investment banking division and its research analysts resulted in a $100 million fine.[26]

In a similar vein, during its fiscal year 2003, according to the SEC, it received penalties and forced the disgorgement of illegal profits to the tune of a combined $2 billion because of its enforcement actions. In 2004, the SEC says this combined amount increased to $3.5 billion.

During 2005, John and Timothy Rigas (John, the father and CEO, and Timothy, the son and CFO) received sentences of fifteen years and twenty years, respectively, for their looting of the cable company Adelphia (now in bankruptcy).

Similarly, in September 2005, a New York state court sentenced Dennis Kozlowski, the former CEO of Tyco International, and Mark Swartz, the former CFO of Tyco, to twenty-five years in a New York state prison as the result of their conviction on a number of counts, including grand larceny and securities fraud. These former executives paid substantial fines and forfeitures: $204 million in the case of Kozlowski, and $35 million in the case of Swartz.

In addition, a New York state trial judge sentenced Bernie Ebbers, the former CEO of WorldCom, to twenty-five years in jail upon his conviction by a New York jury of a number of criminal offenses. Ebbers' offenses relate to the accounting scandals at WorldCom (including securities fraud).

In conclusion, to enumerate all the frauds, deceptive practices, and security frauds during the last five years would require a compendium of treatises. Regardless, business could have prevented most of these by just engaging in the Good Book's principles.

Of course, moving from fraud to good would require conversion by these men to a belief in Jesus Christ as Lord and Savior. Convicted Watergate conspirator Charles Colson turned his life around after such an experience, and we know that two extortionists, the tax collectors Matthew and Zacchaeus, also converted to Christianity. Not only that, Matthew became an apostle of Jesus and the writer of the first gospel of the New Testament.

This book will talk more about the offenses enumerated above later.

BUSINESS TRANSACTIONS

Gamesmanship

In business transactions, the parties play the game on a level playing field. Both sides can hire competent legal counsel and many larger companies have in-house counsel to ensure a company does not enter into bad legal agreements.

Regardless, bad faith can, and does, occur in business transactions. For example, the party with the most gold—the other twisted Golden Rule—often drafts the contract, agreement, note, etc. This draftsmanship would prove no problem except that often the lawyers or executives involved want to play games.

The game consists of drafting a very one-sided agreement with a plethora of restrictive language, indemnifications, representations, warranties, and covenants. The object of the game, in this context, amounts to what the computer called Joshua says in the movie *WarGames*, the object "is to win the game." Winning in this situation amounts to what Covey would call a win-lose proposition.

Winning the game involves purposely making the agreement one-sided so the other side will have to negotiate provisions out. By using this technique, the drafter knows he will get some provisions he absolutely wants and will give up on some he does not want just to appear reasonable in the contract negotiations—as if the other side does not know what he is doing.

This subterfuge results in high legal fees and often frustration on the part of the non-drafting party. It also does not apply scriptural teaching. Under the Biblical Golden Rule, you should treat your neighbor as yourself and no one using this subterfuge could claim he was using the Good Book's rules.

Why shouldn't the drafter just draft a document that's fair to both parties? That's a good question, but there are other ploys beside one-sidedness.

Other ploys include such things as waiting to the last minute—that is, just before the American has to fly back from Europe or Asia—walking out, using a middleman with no authority, verbally lying (so there is no evidence of the lie unless you happen to record the conversation), and playing dumb. Some business people believe the use of such ploys are wise (all's fair in love, war, and business, isn't it?)—the author believes and suggests otherwise. This one-upmanship just delays the process, increases legal fees, and often frustrates the party without the gold.

However, if you were to write a fair contract and play no games then you would achieve a win-win outcome. This does not mean that you do not negotiate those things that are very important to you—just make sure they are important and skip the gamesmanship. To do otherwise results in a win-lose approach that comes about from those utterly selfish people that always have to win.

In addition, such action may prove self-defeating because it does not engender loyalty on the part of the non-drafting party. The use of the technique also suggests the love for money that the Bible proscribes (more about that later).

Good Contract Negotiation

There are some contract provisions that should not render a contract one-sided. For example, a seller usually should not object to certain general hold harmless or indemnification provisions regarding the product sold since any buyer would require them of any seller. Accordingly, the seller should not object to such provisions especially when the seller knows he is selling good products—if the seller does object, remember caveat emptor.

The party borrowing money in a business transaction should not object to monetary default provisions either. After all, the borrower probably also collects money from someone, whether in trade receivables or note receivables, and understands that parties engaged in selling via a note or lending money expect repayment. Actually, the borrower probably has monetary defaults in his own contracts with others and, therefore, expects such provisions.

Regardless, everyone makes mistakes (well, at least their computers do), and the borrower finds that the lender was not paid on time. Borrowers who ask for grace periods or cure periods, after notice, generally get them because lenders understand that mistakes do happen and that a default should not occur unless there is deliberate non-payment. The cost of the mistake is a late fee, again something the borrower understands since they probably also assess late fees on late accounts or notes receivable.

Typical loan documents require that a business borrower provide its lenders with certain documentation, financial statements, or information reports. The lender requires, among other things, such things as monthly unaudited financial statements, annual audited financial statements, collateral reports (e.g., accounts receivable when pledged against a working capital line or property reports for a real estate loan), insurance certificates, and copies of regulatory examination results within specified time periods, whether monthly, quarterly, or annually. Business borrowers generally prepare such reports or financial statements as a matter of course. Generally, the provision of such documents presents the borrower with no hardship.

Similarly, certain corporate events may require notification to the lender. For example, lenders generally want to know about the sale of a majority ownership in the company or the sale of a subsidiary. Such events may even require notification and permission, such as a new credit facility or the sale of assets. Again, the borrower should not find these provisions onerous since they would probably do the same thing if put in the lender's place.

The lender should apply a common sense approach to certain default provisions to ensure fairness. In other words, require the borrower to provide information on a timely basis but do not throw the company into default for minor "foot faults." The loan documents should provide for cure periods for such technical "foot fault" defaults.

Lenders, commonly, desire cross-default provisions for loans within their institution. The borrower should not find such provisions objectionable if coupled with a cure provision.

However, cross-defaults initiated because of a default within another institution are problematic since the lender may find that the borrower's default at the other institution is purely technical and non-monetary. Generally, the loan documents should provide some sort of carve-out for "foot fault" defaults with other lenders—in essence, cross-default only for monetary items.

Similarly, in the case of notice and approval requirements, the lender probably should have those but those provisions should not prevent the borrower from carrying on its usual trade or business. Accordingly, the loan documents should contain a stated period for approval and/or a clause providing something like "permission, which will not be unreasonably withheld" or "deemed approved by bank within thirty days after receipt of notice from borrower of the transaction."[27]

Lenders, also, sometimes ask for inter-creditor agreements, which serve the same purpose as a financing statement. That is, it lets all the lenders know about each other. Generally, this item does not require negotiation; again, the borrower should not object, since if the borrower gets into financial trouble everyone is going to find out anyway.

Further, many treasurers and CFOs of borrowers attempt to limit assertions to what they know. In other words, they want clauses limiting disclosure, representation, or warranty to what they know—the borrower often inserts a clause such as "to the best of his knowledge and belief." Of course, such limitations do not apply to things that the lender would expect the borrower to know—for example, whether the borrower has pledged the collateral elsewhere.

As mentioned previously, some businessmen believe that the person with the gold makes the rules—that is, the party in the greatest position of strength. To put that wrong-headed principle aside, the best way to treat others in a contract is to indeed use the Golden Rule—treat the other contracting party in the same manner as the business likes to be treated.

The basics of contractual etiquette rest upon:

- practicing win-win relationships as suggested by Covey—a win-win approach often creates a partnership and symbiotic relationship
- displaying the utmost in integrity (the Good Book contains a prescriptive rule regarding integrity in the Ten Commandments under the commandment not to lie)—a business builds its reputation and its contractual relationships upon honesty
- keeping your promises (an essential element of contract—again the Good Book covers keeping your promises in a prescriptive rule contained in the Ten Commandments as you shall not lie and in the Lord's statement that "When a man makes a vow to the Lord or takes an oath to obligate himself by a pledge, he

must not break his word but must do everything he said.")[28]

- repaying all favors (if your neighbor treats you kindly you must reciprocate, not just out of common courtesy but because the Lord in the Golden Rule requires it)

FOOTNOTES

[1] A note generally amortizes as the borrower makes payments. This simply means that the payment is sufficient to cover the interest accrued on the loan for a particular period (generally a month). The remainder of the payment over and above the interest due reduces (amortizes) principal. Generally, a lender structures a loan to amortize over a certain period although lenders now commonly make loans with balances due at the end of the loan term (so-called balloon loans). However, if the consumer's loan payment is not sufficient to cover the current interest due then the loan balance will increase—negatively amortize—by the amount of the unpaid interest.

[2] Lev. 19:11 NIV.

[3] Lev. 19:13 NIV.

[4] Lev. 19:15 NIV.

[5] Lev. 25:35 NIV.

[6] Deut. 15:7-11 NIV.

[7] Deut. 24:14 NIV.

[8] Ps. 14:4-6 NIV.

[9] Prov. 14:31 NIV.

[10] Prov. 22:2 NIV.

[11] Prov. 22:22-23 NIV.

[12] Isa. 10:1-2 NIV.

[13] Ezek 22:28-29 NIV.

[14] Amos 5:12-15 NIV.

[15] 2 Cor. 8:8-9 NIV.

[16] Rev. 3:14-18 NIV.

[17] At least, the author knows of none within his laymen's knowledge and experience as a mortgage banker.

[18] The lender could limit his legal liability by appropriate caveats prepared by a competent legal advisor and certain borrower acknowledgments.

[19] 1 Tim. 6:17 NIV.

[20] Prov. 19:17 NIV.

[21] Lev. 25:35 NIV.

[22] James Cameron, "Mortgage Market Trends" (presentation to the MBA Accounting, Tax and Financial Analysis Conference, Las Vegas, NV, November 15, 2004).

[23] Prov 20:17 NIV.

[24] 1 Cor 6:10 NIV.

[25] U.S. Department of Housing and Urban Development, *RESPA - Real Estate Settlement Procedures* Act http://www.hud.gov/offices/hsg/sfh/res/respa_hm.cfm.

[26] David Callahan, *The Cheating Culture: Why More Americans Are Doing Wrong To Get Ahead* (Orlando: Harcourt, Inc., 2004), 6.

[27] The author again reminds the reader that he is not an attorney, is not qualified to provide legal advice, and is not providing it. Rather, these comments are plain sense modifications of contractual documents. The objective of these suggestions is to protect the lender practically rather than legally. In addition, these suggestions go along with the overall purpose of this book; that is, business should apply scriptural principles, including those of fairness, to business transactions.

[28] Num. 30:1-2 NIV.

CHAPTER 7

THE LOVE OF MONEY

The New Testament does not contain any express prohibitions against contracts or the adequacy or inadequacy of consideration. However, the apostle Paul did warn Timothy that the "love of money is the root of all evil" (author's paraphrase, see 1 Ti. 6:10). Paul also warned Timothy that lovers of money could stray from the faith to their own loss—of course, we can see what straying from the path did for Ebbers, the Rigas family, Kozlowski, and Swartz. Similarly, Jesus said, "You cannot serve both God and money"[1] (also see Matthew 6:24).

Even John the Baptist addressed the subject of money. When tax collectors and Roman soldiers came to him after their baptisms, they asked him how they could change their lives. John the Baptist told the tax collectors to collect what they were supposed to collect (see Luke 3:13). As you will remember from previous chapters, the tax collectors often supplemented their earnings by collecting more money from taxpayers than the Roman government told them to collect.

John the Baptist also told the baptized Roman soldiers not to engage in extortion. Again, as with the tax collectors, the Roman soldiers, when the opportunity to supplement their pay through the spoils of wars was lacking, engaged in extortion in the occupied countries or territories, such as Judea, to increase their pay.

Extortion connotes a seedy love of money and, in our society, is usually a crime. Regardless, the extortionist does overly love money and does not want to have to perform a great deal of work to obtain it. John the Baptist told those who suffered from this disease that they needed to stop and to treat people fairly.

Note that many people often misquote Paul's words regarding the love of money. They will say that, "money is the root of all evil" (author's paraphrase) but Paul did not say that. Rather, Paul said that the *"love of money"*[2] (emphasis added) is the root cause of evil and wickedness. Such evil and wickedness includes crime (such as extortion, the sin from which tax collectors and Roman soldiers suffered), miserliness, covetousness, selfishness, envy, fraud, and materialism.

Note that the New Testament implies that the tax collectors suffered from the last sin mentioned above (i.e., materialism—possessing just to possess or the ostentatious display of material possessions to shame your neighbor). The Jews of Palestine in the first century AD not only resented the tax collectors for their wealth and the means they used to acquire it but, also, their ostentatious use and display of that wealth. Remember, that the Pharisees objected to Jesus' attendance at a dinner with the newly converted Matthew because the party included harlots (an illicit and ostentatious use of wealth) and sinners (probably the entourage who openly enjoyed the ill-gotten fruits of Matthew's evil).

Today, as it was in Jesus' day, people often come to the place where their love of money matters more than anything in their lives—including God and family. When money becomes that important to someone, the "love of money"[3] has metamorphosed from a desire for money into a worship of money—in other words, the greenback becomes an idol to such a materialistic person.

In the summer of 2005, this love of money resulted in long

prison sentences for several executives who loved money to the extent that they looted it or stole it from their own companies. For example, a New York state court justice, as previously mentioned, sentenced father and son, John and Timothy Rigas, to fifteen and twenty years, respectively, in state prison. John Rigas was the chief executive officer of Adelphia, a cable company located in New York State. He, in collusion with his son, the chief financial officer, systematically looted the company's coffers as if those coffers were their personal assets.

In another 2005 trial, a jury found two Tyco executives, a CEO and a CFO, guilty of a number of financial crimes and the court sentenced them to twenty-five years each (parole is possible in eight years and four months—1/3 of the sentence). Tyco, the company involved, is still a large operating company with annual revenues exceeding $44 billion. Dennis Kozlowski and Mark Swartz, the former CEO and CFO, were involved in stealing from the company through such things as the forgiveness of loans and fraudulent bonuses. At Mr. Kozlowski's sentencing hearing, an assistant prosecuting district attorney succinctly summed up the case by saying, in referring to Mr. Kozlowski that, "He stole. He committed fraud. He committed perjury."[4] As those who follow the financial news will remember, Kozlowski became infamous for his $2 million toga party for his wife's birthday, his purchase of a $6 thousand dollar shower curtain, and his purchase of an $18 million apartment in New York City.

At around the same time, a New York judge sentenced Bernie Ebbers, former CEO of WorldCom, to twenty-five years in a New York State prison for securities fraud. Mr. Ebbers, who at the time of the writing of this book had posted bond to appeal his sentence, was involved in the $10.7 billion overstatement of the net income of WorldCom during his tenure.

The worship of money, obviously, is a clear violation of

the first commandment, in which God clearly commands man to worship no other god—that is, to put no other god before Him (author's paraphrase of Exod. 20:3). It also is an indirect violation of the tenth commandment regarding coveting because inherently the love of money includes wanting what someone else has.

In a spirit of equanimity, we must point out that there is quite a difference between the love of money and money being the cause of evil. Money is not inherently bad.

For example, anyone that has been poor can tell you without reservation that not having money can result in all types of detrimental consequences including crime, starvation (or at least poor nutrition), frustration, ignorance, disease, and a cycle of continuous poverty. But do not feel that because the United States is the wealthiest nation on earth that we do not have to look for poverty here.

We may find it is easy to point our fingers at the underdeveloped countries in South America, Latin America, Africa, the Middle East, and Asia as examples of the societies that suffer from a lack of money. However, we generally need to look only a relatively short way in any direction to find poverty almost on our doorstep—sometimes it sits just outside the revolving door to our office building.

Interestingly, as Hurricane Katrina swept through New Orleans in 2005, we found that the town of jazz, good food, and good times also contained a very large number of people suffering from the endemic poverty of the very Deep South. For example, the poor make up (or did make up) approximately 28 percent of the population of New Orleans. Other Deep South states have similar problems such as the black belt in Alabama (before one alleges the employment of discriminatory language by the use of this term, they should realize that agronomists call that region of Alabama the black belt because of the type of topsoil found there).

In contrast, we know what good money can bring about.

The Rockefeller, Carnegie, and Gates foundations[5] have all provided money to very worthwhile causes—religious, charitable, educational, scientific, medical, or cultural.

Of course, such giving generally requires an eleemosynary element as opposed to a guilt or public relations element. Eleemosynary is an English word coming from the Latin word meaning alms. Eleemosynary, as with alms, means giving without requiring anything in return and generally reflects a desire to improve and better humanity.

Remember that the root of the English word philanthropy is phileo. Phileo, as you will remember, means to love humanity.

Concerning wealth, Jesus had this to say,

> Do not store up for yourselves treasures on
> earth, where moth and rust destroy, and
> where thieves break in and steal. But store up
> for yourselves treasures in heaven, where
> moth and rust do not destroy, and where
> thieves do not break in and steal. *For where
> your treasure is, there your heart will be also.*[6]
> [Verse numbers omitted and emphasis added.]

In accordance with that wisdom, Henry Ford once sensibly said that, "You can't take your money with you—but you can send it on ahead."[7] Ford meant that you could do unto others today and by so doing you could send your wealth on ahead to heaven.

Jesus would probably agree with Ford. Upon the judgment day of the Gentiles, the King, that is Jesus, will separate the people into two groups—the sheep and the goats. The sheep represent the redeemed and those who will enter the earthly kingdom of Jesus that will last for a millennium (a thousand years). The sheep will also represent those who cared for their fellow men during the tribulation and the King will attribute their good works to good works done *personally* and *specifically* for Him. The King will perplex the sheep when he tells them this—obviously, because they did not ever remember doing anything for the King. They will ask the King, when did we do this for you Lord? The King in reply will say, "I tell you the truth, whatever you did for one of the least of these brothers of mine, you did for me."[8]

When it comes time to judge the goats, those people who loved money more than their fellow man, will find that the King will not know them and will say to them:

> Depart from me, you who are cursed, into the
> eternal fire prepared for the devil and his
> angels. For I was hungry and you gave me
> nothing to eat, I was thirsty and you gave me
> nothing to drink, I was a stranger and you did
> not invite me in, I needed clothes and you
> did not clothe me, I was sick and in prison
> and you did not look after me.[9] [Verse
> numbers omitted.]

The goats will find the King's statement perplexing also for they will not remember ever meeting the King and not doing these things for him. However, the King will reply:

> I tell you the truth, whatever you did not do
> for one of the least of these, you did not do
> for me.

> Then they will go away to eternal
> punishment, but the righteous to eternal
> life.[10] [Verses numbers omitted.]

Although there is some difference of opinion about whom Jesus judges at this time, that difference of opinion is irrelevant because Jesus is consistent and his judgment true. Accordingly, Jesus' treatment of the goats and the sheep will apply at whatever time and to whatever group of people He selects to judge.

Similarly, for those who treat their neighbors wrongly Paul said this:

> Do you not know that the wicked will not inherit the kingdom of God? Do not be deceived: Neither...thieves nor the greedy...nor slanderers nor swindlers will inherit the kingdom of God.[11] [Verse references omitted. Ellipsis material relates primarily to sins of a sexual nature and not to business mores.]

Jesus illustrated the story of the greedy, the dishonest, and the extortionist with a story, which the Bible generally calls a parable. The story, which is only recounted in the gospel of Luke at 16:19-31, involves a rich man who lived the best life one could in the ancient world—he wore purple, which was a sign of wealth because it was an expensive color to produce. He also wore linen, another sign of wealth. He lived in a mansion while Lazarus, a beggar covered with sores, begged outside the house of this unnamed rich man.

Now, if you have ever lived in the Middle East, Africa, or Asia you can easily picture Lazarus. Although the Bible paints a compassionate picture of him, most of us probably would have avoided him. Sores connote leprosy; we would probably have wanted to stay away because of that horrific and disfiguring disease. Further, his overwhelming poverty, which would have included an extremely bad smell, would have probably driven us away even if his other negative characteristics had not.

Of course, I would hope that you would do like the metaphorically described sheep (previously described). That is, I would hope that you would have given him something to drink, food to eat, or clothes to wear but, unfortunately, since we are all sinners, we may have just avoided him.[12]

Jesus did not specifically recount how the rich man accumulated his wealth. Nevertheless, Jesus, by implication, gives us a good idea of how the rich man lived by telling us how he died. Any man's reward or punishment will demonstrate how he used and accumulated his wealth during his lifetime.

Here we find punishment so we can surmise that the rich man was evil during his earthly life for, in this parable, the rich man dies and goes to hell (literally, that is). Since the rich man suffers in the vile setting of hell, the rich man's accumulation of earthly wealth did not result from good business practices but from bad ones.

We do not know what those bad practices were but can only suppose that they were bad because of their consequences to the rich man. At the same time, Lazarus died. Of course, Lazarus was the man who had suffered in his earthly life and whom the rich man had probably looked down upon when he passed him begging at his gate. However, upon Lazarus' death, we have a different result. Lazarus went to heaven.

Obviously, even in a bad earthly situation, Lazarus was a good person. But, again, we do not how he was good or why he deserved a heavenly reward because the Bible does not tell us.

Regardless, we now find the rich man no longer rich and in hell. As Jesus warned us (as quoted above), you cannot take your treasure with you—if he could, the rich man probably would have tried to bribe the devil, which of course would not have worked. As the rich man was suffering in hell he looked up to heaven and saw Abraham and Lazarus—an interesting point of view for one who looked down on others when he lived on earth.

Now the rich man had to look up because he was the person of low standing—a standing more important than his earthly one. Upon looking up, he saw Lazarus with whom he was familiar, since Lazarus during his earthly life had frequented the rich man's gate as a beggar.

Now the rich man who was indeed suffering simply asked Abraham for some water just to cool his tongue—a very small request. He also asked Abraham if Lazarus could bring him the water needed to cool his tongue.

In response, Abraham refused. Abraham indicated that Lazarus could not bring the water because of the gulf that separated heaven and hell. Abraham also plainly reminded the rich man that he had enjoyed his pleasure on earth and now it was time for Lazarus to enjoy his pleasure. Ironically, the rich man had trusted in wealth that moth and rust could destroy and that lasted for a very short and finite period. On the other hand, in comparison to the rich man's finite earthly enjoyment Lazarus' enjoyment would last forever.

The rich man, upon receiving Abraham's refusal, became concerned about his brothers, and he asked Abraham to send Lazarus to warn his brothers of their potential[13] fate. Presumably, the rich man's brothers engaged in the same wicked business practices of the rich man—they may have even been partners. Because of the wicked business practices (whatever they were), the former rich man's brothers would probably share same the same fate as their dead brother. In other words, God, because of their greedy and evil earthly actions, had given them a "do not pass go card." In other words, the brothers were also going to hell because of their actions on earth.

Again, Abraham refused the former rich man's request. In reply, Abraham essentially told the rich man that his brothers had the Bible and the prophets. Both the Bible and the prophets warned of the consequences of their nefarious earthly business practices and they knew those consequences. Further, Abraham did not feel that even the resurrection of a dead man would change their behavior. In other words, you shall receive your appropriate reward whether it is now or later.

Now if you think a dead man's resurrection would always change someone's behavior and that the witnesses would then turn to God, you are, regrettably, wrong. You see there were two resurrections of the dead that did not change people's minds. One, the resurrection of Lazarus of Bethany (another Lazarus who was neither poor nor a beggar), only strengthened the resolve of the Pharisees to kill Jesus— strange behavior if you were to canvas most people. Nevertheless, the Pharisees hated Jesus more after He resurrected Lazarus of Bethany. Similarly, the resurrection of Jesus, the Pharisees tried to explain His Resurrection away by accusing a) the Roman soldiers of falling asleep outside the tomb—a failure that carried the death penalty for a Roman soldier—and b) the disciples of stealing the body away while the Roman soldiers slept. Of course, we know that most of the disciples, before they became aware of the resurrection, were hiding out in fear of the authorities (the thought of hanging on a cross can do that to someone because crucifixion was such a horrible way to die).

The parable of Lazarus the beggar might confuse you since this book has stated that God does not base salvation on works but on grace (See Eph 2:8-10). Some have even turned the doctrine of salvation by grace into heresy by accepting a strange doctrine that the Lord allows one to engage in any behavior once a person repents and is born again.

For example, the antinomians (from the Latin and Greek, meaning anti-law) believed that you could engage in any behavior for God's salvation is sufficient to cover any sin. In this regard, *Merriam-Webster's Collegiate Dictionary* describes an antinomian as "one who holds that under the gospel dispensation of grace the moral law is of no use or obligation because faith alone is necessary to salvation."[14] As you can see, this is a strange belief.

However, Paul fought this heresy in the Philippian church by saying:

> For, as I have often told you before and now say again even with tears, many live as enemies of the cross of Christ. Their destiny is destruction, their god is their stomach, and their glory is in their shame. Their mind is on earthly things.[15] [Verse numbers omitted.]

Further, Paul said in Ephesians 2:10 (the verse that people often overlook when they quote the preceding two verses of that chapter dealing with salvation through grace and not of works) that: "For we are God's workmanship, created in Christ Jesus to do good works, which God prepared in advance for us to do."[16]

In other words, once you accept Christ as Lord and Savior, then you will want to do good works. Otherwise, as the apostle James suggests in his epistle, you may not have found salvation and, accordingly, will continue in the world's evil ways. To wit:

> Do not merely listen to the word, and so deceive yourselves. Do what it says. Anyone who listens to the word but does not do what it says is like a man who looks at his face in a mirror and, after looking at himself, goes away and immediately forgets what he looks like.[17]

As some teachers are wont to say, let a word to the wise be

sufficient. Or, as Mark Twain said, "Always do right. It will gratify some people and astonish the rest."[18]

FOOTNOTES

[1] Luke 16:13 NIV.

[2] 1 Tim. 6:10 NIV.

[3] Ibid.

[4] The Associated Press and staff reporter Mark Maremont, "Kozlowski, Swartz Sentenced to Up to 25 Years in Prison", *The Wall Street Journal Online*, September 19, 2005, U.S. Business News.

[5] Interestingly, John D. Rockefeller Sr. was a monopolist who became very rich through unfair and deceptive practices. Ironically, he left some of his ill-gotten gains for the benefit of humanity.

[6] Matt. 6:19-21 NIV.

[7] Paul Lee Tan, *Encyclopedia of 7700 Illustrations: A Treasury of Illustrations, Anecdotes, Facts and Quotations for Pastors, Teachers and Christian Workers* (Garland, TX: Bible Communications, 1996), s.v. "Epigram on Rewards, Henry Ford."

[8] Matt. 25:40 NIV.

[9] Matt. 25:41-43 NIV.

[10] Matt. 25:45-46 NIV.

[11] 1 Co 6:9-10 NIV.

[12] "For all have sinned and fall short of the glory of God." Rom. 3:23 NIV.

[13] The word potential is used here because a man up to his dying breath has the opportunity to accept Jesus Christ as Lord and Savior. Although this is theoretically possible it becomes increasingly improbable the older one gets.

[14] *Merriam-Webster's Collegiate dictionary*, 10th ed., s.v. "antinomian."

[15] Phil. 3: 18-19 NIV.

[16] Eph. 2:10 NIV.

[17] James 1:22-25 NIV.

[18] Tan, s.v., "Integrity in Life, Epigram on Mark Twain's Motto."

CHAPTER 8

BUSINESS ETHICS

Omar Bradley, the famous American general of the Second World War, said: "We have grasped the mystery of the atom and rejected the Sermon on the Mount....The world has achieved brilliance without conscience. Ours is a world of nuclear giants and ethical infants."[1] For a Christian, this is an apt description of the state of ethics in American business and society as we begin the twenty-first century.

Some call ethics "moral philosophy."[2] In that sense it means, the study of what is good, right, and equitable. *Webster's* applies these denotations to the word:

> 1 ...the discipline dealing with what is good
> and bad and with moral duty and
> obligation[,]
> 2 a : a set of moral principles or values[,]
>   b : a theory or system of moral values...[,]
>   c ...the principles of conduct governing an
>   individual or a group...[and,]
>   d : a guiding philosophy

Interestingly, this definition of ethics corresponds very closely to what Carter defines as integrity. As you will remember, Carter, a Yale law professor, defines integrity in terms of discerning what is right and wrong, walking the walk, and talking the talk. Regardless, we will discuss ethics in the more traditional sense. However, with that said, we assert that integrity is the cornerstone of any system of ethics or moral philosophy—at least to a Christian.

In business, although business ethics do deal with what is right or good and most of the time addresses integrity, ethics in business means different things to its various segments. For instance, in the case of a profession, ethics refers to a code or to standards of conduct. Conversely, in the case of a business, ethics refers to acceptable business practices.

You can recognize the difference by understanding that most codes of ethics for professionals (those that Waylon Jennings and Willie Nelson call "doctors and lawyers and such" in the song "Mammas Don't Let Your Babies Grow Up To Be Cowboys") include some form of declaration of responsibility to those the profession serves. In contrast, a business code of ethics spells out the practices and conduct a company expects of its employees. Codes of ethics for professions are profession specific, while business codes of ethics are generally company specific.

ETHICS AND THE OLD TESTAMENT

Interestingly, Achtemeier (author of *Harper's Bible Dictionary*) connects wisdom (one of the primary topics of this book and the Old Testament) and ethics. Achtemeier defines wisdom in reference to ethical conduct and supports his assertion with reference to the second Chapter of Proverbs. Proverbs 2:9-11 says when wisdom comes:

> Then you will understand what is right and just and fair—every good path. For wisdom will enter your heart, and knowledge will be pleasant to your soul. Discretion will protect you, and understanding will guard you.[3]
> [Verses omitted.]

Of course, as the other chapters of this book emphasize, the Old Testament provides various ethical standards. As explained earlier, the Jews initially had no ethical underpinnings and through the Law the Lord provided them with one. Most of those ethical teachings are found in the law (the Torah, the first five books of the Old Testament) or in the books of Proverbs, Psalms, or Ecclesiastes. Although much of the latter three books deal with wisdom, the author of this book agrees with Achtemeier and believes that wisdom and ethics are intertwined.

THE NEW TESTAMENT AND ETHICS

Commentators often point to the Sermon on the Mount contained in Matthew 5-7 and in Luke 6:20-49 as the ethical teaching of Jesus.[4] Here we find recounted both the world's Golden Rule and Jesus' Golden Rule. Jesus enunciated His Golden Rule as a rejoinder to the world's rule.

> You have heard that it was said, "Love your neighbor and hate your enemy." [Here Jesus enunciates the world's viewpoint— immediately following is his rejoinder.] But I tell you: Love your enemies and pray for those who persecute you, that you may be sons of your Father in heaven. He causes his sun to rise on the evil and the good, and sends rain on the righteous and the unrighteous. If you love those who love you, what reward will you get? Are not even the tax collectors doing that? And if you greet only your brothers, what are you doing more than others? Do not even pagans do that? Be perfect, therefore, as your heavenly Father is

perfect.[5] [Verse references and footnotes omitted—minor changes made for style of quoted material—inserts made by the author.]

The word perfect as used here does need some clarification. The connotation in this explication is not of a person that is unblemished, without sin, or pure. Rather, as Jamieson, Fausset, and Brown explain in A Commentary, Critical and Explanatory, on the Old and New Testaments, the word implies the goal a disciple should strive for—that is, the disciple should strive for excellence just as the Lord is excellent.

A NEW EMPHASIS ON BUSINESS ETHICS

It seems like there are accounting scandals everywhere. The Economist in a 2002 article[6] pointed out that that some 250 American public companies [restated]…their accounts… [in 2001], compared with only 92 in 1997 and three in 1981." In the same vein, Harry Pitts, former Chairman of the Securities and Exchange Commission (SEC), in testimony to Congress in 2003 pointed out that in 2002, the SEC had increased its enforcement actions.

> For the fiscal year through August 20, 2003, the Commission has filed 543 enforcement actions, 147 of which involve financial fraud or reporting violations. During this period, the Commission has sought to bar 144 offending corporate executives and directors from holding such positions with publicly traded companies.[7]

During its fiscal year 2003, according to the SEC, it received penalties and forced the disgorgement of illegal profits to the tune of a combined $2 billion because of its enforcement actions.[8] In 2004, the SEC reported that this combined amount increased to $3.5 billion.[9]

These statistics reveal the amount of accounting shenanigans going on in industry. These statistics may have proved surprising to some public company observers but not to the more cynical and more skeptical observers among them.

Even some very large, well-known, and visible companies engaged in unethical accounting practices. Of course, the more cynical and skeptical, especially those that have studied business history, remember that a lack of *enforcement*[10] and guidance[11] often results in egregious behavior by large companies. For example, we only have to look to the business tycoons and the trusts of the late nineteenth century and the stock market crash of 1929 for some very cogent and pertinent examples.

The accounting scandals at Enron and WorldCom are credited with Congress passing the Sarbanes-Oxley Act of 2002 (Sarbanes-Oxley). However, Enron and WorldCom are not the only culprits. For example, other companies such as Xerox, AIG Insurance, Adelphia, HealthSouth, Tyco, Marsh & McLennan, Coca-Cola Co., Freddie Mac, and Fannie Mae, among scores of others, have also been involved in accounting overstatements or deceptive practices, resulting in a new emphasis on corporate ethics.

Interestingly, Section 406 of Sarbanes-Oxley requires a public company (a company with securities registered in the public markets, which can be bonds or stocks) to disclose whether it has a code of ethics for the senior financial officers of a company. Section 406 does not require that a company have such a code, because the federal government does not have the power to prescribe certain rules for corporations since under our federal system such powers are reserved to the states. Rather, Section 406 only requires the company disclose whether it has such a code or not and, if it does not have such a code, then the company must explain why it does not.

The SEC by regulation extended the application of the code of conduct rules to the principal executive officer of a company as well. In addition, a company must disclose any change or waiver of this policy in a Form 8-K filing (a form 8-K relates to significant events a company should disclose to the public and the SEC, such as a major sale of part of its business).

Of course, the Section 406 disclosure rules means that a company will have a code of ethics for its CEO and principal accounting officers. After all, who wants to disclose that they do not have a code of ethics? The explanation of "why not" would be hard enough in itself to provide—justifiable and valid reasons for not doing so appear to be close to zero. Further, the investment community would probably question the ethics and motives of any company who decided it did not need a code of ethics for its financial officers and its principal executive officer (as an aside you would also have to wonder about their smarts or, more specifically, the lack of such).

The federal government and its agencies have provided other reasons for creating and enforcing codes of ethics. In what some call to the "carrot approach"[12] to complying with the law, the federal sentencing guidelines (in case you get in trouble with the federal government) provide for the amelioration of fines, penalties, and sentences if a company has a code of ethics, the company monitors compliance with the code, and the company enforces the code. Similarly, the SEC also provides for such amelioration in its guidelines for settlements with those that violate the U.S. securities laws.

Example of a 406 Disclosure and a Code of Ethics for the CEO and the Company's Principal Accounting Officers

As an example of the Sarbanes-Oxley 406 disclosure, the 2005 Form 10-K of Cisco Systems, Inc. (the 10-K is the SEC's annual report form) states that:

> We have adopted a code of ethics that applies to our principal executive officer and all members of our finance department, including the principal financial officer and principal accounting officer. This code of ethics, which consists of the "Special Ethics Obligations for Employees with Financial Reporting Responsibilities" section of our Code of Business Conduct that applies to employees generally, is posted on our Website.

An extract of Cisco's Code of Conduct for its principal executive officer and senior financial officers follows.

> Because of this special role, the Chief Executive Officer and all members of Cisco's Finance Department are bound by the following Financial Officer Code of Ethics, and by accepting the Code of Business Conduct, each agrees that he or she will, in his or her capacity as an employee of Cisco:
>
> *Act with honesty and integrity, avoiding actual or apparent conflicts of interest*

in personal and professional relationships.

Provide information that is accurate, complete, objective, relevant, timely, and understandable to ensure full, fair, accurate, timely, and understandable disclosure in reports and documents that Cisco files with, or submits to, government agencies and in other public communications.

Comply with rules and regulations of federal, state, provincial and local governments, and other appropriate private and public regulatory agencies.

Act in good faith, responsibly, with due care, competence and diligence, without misrepresenting material facts or allowing his or her independent judgment to be subordinated.

Respect the confidentiality of information acquired in the course of his or her work except when authorized or otherwise legally obligated to disclose. *Confidential information acquired in the course of his or her work will not be used for personal advantage.*

Share knowledge and *maintain skills important and relevant to stakeholder's needs.*

Proactively promote and be an example of ethical behavior as a responsible partner among peers, in the work environment and the community.

Achieve responsible use of and control over all assets and resources employed or entrusted.

Promptly report to the Director of Internal Control Services and/or the Chairman of the Audit Committee *any conduct that the individual believes to be a violation of law or business ethics or of any provision of the Code of Conduct,* including any transaction or relationship that reasonably could be expected to give rise to such a conflict.

Violations of this Financial Officer Code of Ethics, including failures to report potential violations by others, *will be viewed as a severe disciplinary matter that may result in personnel action, including termination of employment.*[13] [Emphasis added.]

PROFESSIONAL ETHICAL STANDARDS

Some examples will illustrate the declarations of responsibility generally issued by professional societies or organizations. As discussed previously, one of the primary differences in a professional code of conduct and a business code of conduct is a declaration of responsibility.

The code of conduct for accountants as expressed by the American Institute of Certified Public Accountants states:

> These Principles of the Code of Professional Conduct of the American Institute of Certified Public Accountants express the profession's recognition of *its responsibilities to the public, to clients, and to colleagues.*[14] [Emphasis added.]

The code of conduct for realtors as expressed by the National Association of Realtors® states:

> When representing a buyer, seller, landlord, tenant, or other client as an agent, Realtors® *pledge themselves to protect and promote the interests of their client. This obligation to the client is primary, but it does not relieve Realtors® of their obligation to treat all parties honestly.*[15] [Emphasis added.]

The code of conduct for journalists as expressed by the Society of Professional Journalists states:

> Members of the Society of Professional Journalists believe that public enlightenment is the forerunner of justice and the foundation of democracy. The duty of the journalist is to further those ends by seeking truth and providing a fair

and comprehensive account of events and issues. *Conscientious journalists from all media and specialties strive to serve the public with thoroughness and honesty.*[16]

The code of conduct for attorneys as expressed by the American Bar Association states:

> a) …, a lawyer shall abide by a client's decisions concerning the objectives of representation and, …, shall consult with the client as to the means by which they are to be pursued. A lawyer may take such action on behalf of the client as is impliedly authorized to carry out the representation. A lawyer shall abide by a client's decision whether to settle a matter. In a criminal case, the lawyer shall abide by the client's decision, after consultation with the lawyer, as to a plea to be entered, whether to waive jury trial and whether the client will testify.[17] [References to other paragraphs omitted.]

In addition, professional standards include such things as the professional's responsibilities involving due care, competence, confidentiality, non-discrimination, legal compliance, conflicts of interest, independence, objectivity, and integrity. Note that the Cisco's Financial Officer Code of Ethics includes many of those same things.

As mentioned above, a business code of ethics generally deals with acceptable business practices, which are primarily concerned with *what is good for the business.* Paradoxically, as more fully discussed in a following section, *what is good for the business often proves good for society.*

With the passage of Sarbanes-Oxley, as discussed above, certain parts of a public company's code of ethics deal with compliance with the securities laws and concomitantly with the protection of shareholder interests (stakeholders). However, most codes of ethics serve as an internal control tool, which allows the company to achieve certain business control objectives, including such functional categories as operations, performance, financial reporting, and compliance.

Some build their code of ethics around certain corporate core values as Collins and Porras define that term in their book, *Built to Last, Successful Habits of Visionary Companies.* Core values to Collins and Porras consist of those ethical values (or mores) a company believes will allow the company to achieve its stated purpose (other than just making money). They say it this way: "Core values are the organization's essential and enduring tenets, not to be compromised for financial gain or short-term expediency."[18]

Corporate codes of ethics include many of the same things that professional codes of ethics (or standards of conduct) address, including integrity, conflicts of interests, confidentiality, non-discrimination, and legal compliance. However, a business code of ethics will probably address things a professional association would not since the codes serve different people and a business creates its code of ethics for a different purpose. The professional serves his client while a business, in the general sense, serves its customers and owes duties to its vendors, employees, and stakeholders.

The professional may also owe duties to such parties but his professional standards are designed to assure that service to his client is paramount. Moreover, although a business may provide services, those services generally differ from those of a professional. Services provided by a profession generally require certain types of training, qualification tests, service periods, licensure, and activity restrictions.

In contrast, a business code of ethics may include such things as:

- restricting nepotism or the supervision of family members
- complying with anti-trust provisions (remember the Sherman Anti-Trust Act and the Clayton Act previously described)
- complying with the securities laws and regulations of the security regulators (e.g., insider trading prohibition and required disclosure when certain sales of corporate stock occur)
- restricting political activities
- ensuring regulatory compliance (for example, security broker-dealers, food companies, drug companies, investment advisors, financial institutions, insurance companies, and public utilities all face different regulatory regimes and requirements)
- prohibiting the personal use of company assets
- protecting company assets
- proscribing gifts to vendors or government officials
- proscribing bribes
- complying with fair business practices
- prohibiting bid rigging
- requiring certain employment practices (e.g., non-discrimination, equal opportunity, and non-sexual harassment)

- limiting or prohibiting gifts or favors
- encouraging independence in vendor and contractual relationships (e.g., not doing business with related parties)
- prohibiting kickbacks
- ensuring the health and safety of company employees
- providing bidding rules
- defining appropriate vendor interaction
- protecting trade secrets and intellectual property
- prohibiting controlled substance use
- ensuring environmental law compliance
- avoiding money laundering
- remaining neutral in international trade relations
- encouraging fair dealing
- avoiding deceptive practices

All of the above met certain legal, regulatory, employee relations, business, and ethical norms. They are all ethical in that they provide for fairness, justice, and honesty and differentiate between what is right or wrong.

GOOD BUSINESS PRACTICES

Regardless of the legal requirements or the reasons for providing a code of ethics, Collins and Porras suggest in *Built to Last* that companies with *working* sets of codes of ethics or core values include the more successful companies. But, this means more than having the core values written down— that's why the author stressed the adjective *working* in the description of what Collins and Porras find in regards to core values. In other words, those companies that *applied* the practices they espoused were more likely to be successful. That is, as Carter suggests, they walk the walk.

Unfortunately, as Callahan points out in the chapter titled "Temptation Nation," contained in his book, *The Cheating Culture, Why More Americans are Doing Wrong to Get Ahead*, even those who purport to be Christians can fail to walk the walk. Although I do not know these individuals, and the following statement is pure supposition, you would have to wonder whether the admonition of Apostle James applies to those who recently failed God in applying the Good Book's principles. As you will remember James says, "Do what [scripture] says."[19]

Callahan points out that Ebbers, of WorldCom fame, is an evangelistic Christian and a Baptist. Callahan also says that John Rigas, founder of Adelphia Communications, and his sons, are Greek Orthodox, and purportedly extolled very conservative and ethical values and were stalwart conservative leaders in their community. Further, Callahan asserts that Philip Anschutz, the founder of Qwest Communications who engaged in illegal insider trading while running that company, portrayed himself as a Christian. Further, Anschutz monetarily supported some Christian non-profit organizations at the same time (hopefully, without his ill-gotten gains but it would be hard to tell since money is fungible).[20]

However, the business and Christian failures of these men should not result in an illogical conclusion, a tautology. That is, Christians run big companies, big companies have ethical problems, therefore, Christians running big companies are unethical. We only have a limited number of cases out of a total of approximately 8,800 public companies so positive correlation probably does not exist.

Of course, we know that our society hides from view those Christians managers who do good things, and who are ethical—our society seems to focus on the bad rather than the good. Just like the good CEOs mentioned by Collins in *Good to Great* those Christians often operate in the background.

Our free press and we Americans are more interested in the bad that men do than the good they do (although we do occasionally like a good human-interest story). As Mark Antony said in Shakespeare's play, *Julius Caesar*, we oft inter the good with a good man's bones (author's paraphrase).

Collins and Porras also found that companies with a *working* core ideology prove visionary (a core ideology equals a company's core values plus the company's sound and underlying core purposes). Of course, in the view of Collins and Porras, visionary companies are the more successful companies, which their research in *Built to Last* proved.

Although altruism through a set of moral and societal beneficial core values may seem goody two-shoes, such values often come from the sincere religious, ethical, and moral beliefs of a company's founder (take ACIPCO's Eagan for example). A study of the history of Ford Motor Company reveals that Henry Ford is one of those that provided such core values (although his company departed from such values for a while). Ford provided his employees producing the Ford Model T with a living wage (also noted by Collins and Porras). Paradoxically, this increase in wages came from a man, Ford, who could have justifiably insisted that the worker deserved less because with the implementation of the assembly line the worker was less skilled.

However, Henry Ford's desire to provide his employees with a living wage resulted in people that could afford to buy the car he made. Furthermore, although this is supposition, it probably provided them the incentive to produce Model T more efficiently and reliably. Consequently, Ford profited from what many at the time thought a ruinous business practice.[21]

Collins and Porras provide another example of the benefit

that this so-called altruism can produce. In this example, Merck (a company that has recently received negative publicity from its recall of the drug Vioxx) provided streptomycin, an anti-bacterial drug, to Japan gratis after the end of World War II. This kindness not only produced heavenly rewards for the company executives who implemented the decision (remember doing good things for someone is the same as doing it for the King), but produced a large market share for Merck products in Japan because the Japanese remembered the good deed done for them.[22]

Moreover, this was true kindness. Remember that the Japanese were an occupied people at that time and a recent enemy (one who had started a war with a pre-emptive surprise attack on Pearl Harbor). Japan was an enemy that had committed many war crimes in China and Korea and against American prisoners of war as well.

Regardless, Merck applied Jesus' Sermon on the Mount principles when they gave the streptomycin to the Japanese (something they could have easily justified not doing to an enemy that had probably killed or wounded many Merck employees). However, Merck did as Jesus said. As you will remember, Jesus commanded that you "…love your enemies, do good to them, and lend to them without expecting to get anything back."[23]

FOOTNOTES

[1] Federer, s.v., "Bradley, Omar Nelson."

[2] Encyclopedia Britannica 2006 Ultimate Reference Suite CD, s.v. "ethics."

[3] Prov. 2:9-11 NIV.

[4] The Sermon on the Mount is referred to the Sermon on the Plains in Luke.

[5] Matt.: 5:43-48 NIV.

[6] *The Economist*, (November 28, 2002).

[7] Senate Committee on Banking, Housing and Urban Affairs, *Testimony Concerning Implementation of the Sarbanes-Oxley Act of 2002 William H. Donaldson Chairman U.S. Securities and Exchange Commission*, September 9, 2003.

[8] United States Securities and Exchange Commission, *SEC 2003 Annual Report*.

[9] United States Securities and Exchange Commission, *In Brief*, "Fiscal 2006, Congressional Budget Request," February 2005.

[10] It is interesting that the SEC beefed up its enforcement staff after the market had found out about all the unethical business practices and, then, only when Congress increased the SEC's funding in response to the magnitude and number of such failings in the business community. It is also ironic, at least to the cynic, that Congress increased the SEC's budget only after the stock market suffered a crisis of confidence and the failure of two very large companies. As asserted previously, government does not seem to do a very good job of prevention but does seem to overreact very well—although too often to the extreme. However, the danger is that government will again become complacent; the SEC will become an easy target for Congressional budget cutters; and then we will have to go through this all over again. Nofsinger and Kim in *Infectious Greed* point out that in many ways the public company crises of the twenty-first century mirror those of the 1920s and 1930s. For example, in Chapter 10, "The Securities and Exchange Commission," they describe the environment of the 1920s, which mirrors the twenty-first century quite closely.

[11] It is, however, very difficult to argue that current companies lack guidance in this area since most of the laws have existed for sixty to seventy years—you would think they would have got it by now.

[12] Dove Izraeli and Mark S. Schwartz, "What Can We Learn From the U.S. Federal Sentencing Guidelines for Organizational Ethics?" (paper to the European Institute for Business Ethics, n.d.).

[13] Cisco Systems, Inc., *Cisco Code of Business Conduct*, http://media.corporate-ir.net/media_files/IROL/81/81192/corpgov/codeofconduct_050404_final.pdf

[14] American Institute of Certified Public Accountants, *Code of Professional Conduct of the American Institute of Certified Public Accountants*, (New York: AICPA, 2005).

[15] National Association of Realtors, *Code of Ethics and Standards of Practice of the National Association of Realtors®*, (Washington, D.C., National Association of Realtors, 2005).

[16] Society of Professional Journalists, *Code of Ethics* (Indianapolis, IN: Society of Professional Journalists, 2005)

[17] American Bar Association, Center for Professional Responsibility, *Compendium of Client Protection Rules* (Chicago: ABA Publishing, 2005).

[18] James C. Collins and Jerry I. Porras, *Built to Last, Successful Habits of Visionary Companies* (New York: HarperCollins, 1997), 73.

[19] James 1:22 NIV.

[20] David Callahan, *The Cheating Culture, Why More Americans are Doing Wrong to Get Ahead* (Orlando: Harcourt, Inc., 2004), 136-138.

[21] Collins and Porras, 52-53.

[22] Collins and Porras, 47.

[23] Luke 6:35 NIV.

CHAPTER 9

HE'LL BE THERE

I have taught and I feel that Christianity is one of the hardest religions in the world to practice. Christianity's difficulties come about because it is a religion of "do's" rather than "don'ts."

Some may disagree with my contention that Christianity is a religion of doing. Many Christians of today, and of yesteryear, emphasize the "don'ts" as in "don't do this" or "don't that."

"Don'ts" are inherently negative. On the other hand, Jesus, except when addressing the religious hypocrisy of the first century, Common Era, was positive in telling you what you should do rather than what not to do.

The Old Testament and the epistles of Paul are full of "don'ts" and it is easy to understand why some Christians believe that Christianity is a religion of "don'ts." However, Jesus, who is the fulfillment of the Old Testament prophecies, emphasized the positive of doing God's will through proactive action—both of the two most important commandments (love God and love your neighbor), according to Jesus, involve proactive action rather than prohibition on man's actions.

God himself displayed positive treatment toward individuals throughout the Bible, even when they did not deserve it. For example, why did God pick Abraham from all the pagans inhabiting Mesopotamia? Well, obviously, because of God's love of Abraham and Abraham's faith in God—neither of which is negative. When God called Abraham, the

Law did not exist and there were no "don'ts" (those came later with Moses). God's acceptance of Abraham did not come from anything Abraham had done because there was no way for Abraham to have known what to do.

God picked Abraham because God loved him and because he accepted God's love, and because he stepped out on faith when God called him—all positive and proactive actions. In other words, as Paul said in Romans, Abraham did not have anything to boast about—he simply accepted God's gift of love for him (see Romans 3 and 4).

As the result of Abraham's relationship with God and his faith in God, God promised to create a great nation from Abraham's seed. God honored this promise when He picked Moses to lead the Hebrews from Egypt during the Exodus. He also honored the promise by not forsaking a very disagreeable, apostate, ungrateful, complaining, and undisciplined Hebrew nation. God keeping His covenant (or contract) with Abraham is one the most vivid displays of His proactive love for undeserving, sinful man.

God also demonstrated a number of other proactive "do's" in both the New and Old Testament—"do's" that are very easy to understand. I have often said that God's theology is very simple and consists of such things as loving God, practicing the Golden Rule, caring for widows and orphans, continually learning, acquiring wisdom, sharing the Good News (the Gospel), helping the poor, and not loving money. All of those commandments are contained in uncomplicated, declarative sentences that even the Christian layman can understand. The difficulty rests in the application of those scriptures.

The difficulty comes because the "do's" require that we let go of ourselves and put others ahead of ourselves and that is contrary to man's inherent, selfish nature. As Maslowe theorizes, man by nature must satisfy his basic needs (food, shelter, protection, and procreation) before he can move on to his supplemental needs (the needs for God, recognition, learning, and love).

As I understand Maslowe, he would place the need for God in man's supplemental needs category, but before you get mad and say that God should come first (as He should), follow my discussion and read on. Man's basic instincts drive him to satisfy his primal needs, according to Maslowe, before he can move on to any higher intellectual, societal, economic, or religious calling. It is difficult for a starving man to pursue any higher part of his nature because he must first satisfy the hunger.

The drive for satisfaction of his primal needs is always within a man even when he is not hungry or homeless. The presence of those basic needs is what makes man selfish—he cannot help it or escape his self-interest; his basic instincts for survival necessitate that those needs predominate.

The survival instinct and the need to satisfy his basic needs makes man concentrate on himself and his immediate family (remember that one of man's basic needs includes continuing his line through reproduction). Unrepentant man is, therefore, always concerned with himself—in other words, he is innately concerned with "I" and "me" rather than "you," "us," or "them." I have often told my Sunday School classes to remember that "I" is right in the middle of S-*I*-N. "I" is also right in the middle of P-R-*I*-D-E, a manifestation of putting "me" first.

Sin and pride both result from selfishness and a turning away from God and his precepts and requirements. Scofield refers to sin as "missing the mark"—that is falling short of God's divine requirements. However, I believe the Good Book requires that I put God first, you second, and me third, although sin and pride always want to put "me" before God and "you."

In contrast, the Good Book flips our selfish hierarchy of needs on its head and consistently asserts that God comes first, and then your neighbor. As you will remember, Jesus told the lawyer (or scribe) that God's two greatest commandments consist of the commands to first love God and then love man, your neighbor.

I have often asked my Sunday School classes: Who comes first in your life? I typically receive the classic Sunday School responses—that is, God or Jesus. Then I ask them to think about that answer: Do you really put God and Jesus first?

I know that I often do not. As a CPA, during busy season, I have often put work before Jesus and I admit that I have worked on Sundays to finish audits or tax returns. Even when I served as an executive or manager in industry, I would forget about loving my neighbor and would lose my temper with my subordinates simply because I put myself before them.

I, like Paul, am the worst among sinners but as explained in a footnote to Chapter 4, "Your Most Important Asset," I, like other Christians, try to put God first and repent when I fail Him. I know in His compassionate love that He forgives me, although I often do not think I am worthy of such forgiveness.

This admission of failure is a central tenet of this book on the Good Book and good business. Even though we will fail in our attempts to follow the path that God lays out for us, we should attempt, nevertheless, to follow the "do's" of God's commandments. In the work place, God wants us to continue to try to apply his "do's." Further, he will help us do so if we:

- put Him first and love Him
- tirelessly look to Him for guidance through prayer and study of His word
- repent when we fail Him
- seek His wisdom
- apply His love
- not let failure dissuade us from His prescribed courses of action

If we try to apply His principles of wisdom and love to our dealing with our employees, our customers, our vendors, our investors, and our leaders, He will be there to help us and will pick us up when we stumble and fall. In a paraphrase of a popular song, "He'll be there."

BIBLIOGRAPHY

Achtemeier, Paul J. *Harper's Bible Dictionary*. San Francisco: Harper & Row, 1985.

American Sermons: The Pilgrims to Martin Luther King Jr. New York, New York: The Library of America, 1999.

Barclay, William. *Daily Study Bible Series*. Rev. ed. 17 vols. Philadelphia, Pennsylvania: The Westminster Press, 1975-1976.

Barker, Kenneth L. and John Kohlenberger III. *Zondervan NIV Bible Commentary*. 2 vols. Grand Rapids, Michigan: Zondervan Publishing House, 1994.

Black, Henry Campbell. *Black's Law Dictionary*. Abridged 6th ed. St. Paul, Minn.: West Publishing Co., 1991.

Bonhoeffer, Dietrich. *Ethics*. First Touchstone ed. New York, NY: Simon & Schuster, 1995.

Brandenburger, Adam M. and Barry J. Nalebuff. *Co-opetition*. New York, New York: Currency Doubleday, 1996.

Callahan, David. *The Cheating Culture: Why More Americans Are Doing Wrong to Get Ahead*. Orlando, Florida: Harcourt, Inc., 2004.

Carter, Stephen L. *Integrity*. New York: BasicBooks, 1996.

Collins, James C. *Good to Great: Why Some Companies Make the Leap and Others Don't*. New York, NY: HarperBusiness, 2001.

Collins, James C. and Jerry I. Porras. *Built to Last: Successful Habits of Visionary Companies*. New York: HarperBusiness, 1997.

Covey, Stephen R. *Principle-Centered Leadership*. New York: Simon & Schuster, 1992.

_____. *The Seven Habits of Highly Effective People: Restoring the Character Ethic*. New York: Simon & Schuster, 1990.

Covey, Stephen R., A. Roger Merrill, and Rebecca R. Merrill.

First Things First: To Live, To Love, To Learn, To Leave a Legacy. New York: Simon & Schuster, 1995.

Das, Lama Surya. *Awakening the Buddha Within.* (New York: Broadway Books, 1997)

Downes, John and Jordan Elliot Goodman. *Dictionary of Finance and Investment Terms.* 5th ed. Hauppauge, NY: Barron's Educational Series, Inc., 1998.

Drucker, Peter. *Managing in Turbulent Times.* New York: HarperCollins Publishers, 1993.

Easton, M.G. *Easton's Bible Dictionary.* Oak Harbor, WA: Logos Research Systems, Inc., 1996.

Federer, William J. *Great Quotations: A Collection of Passages, Phrases, and Quotations Influencing Early and Modern World History Referenced According to Their Sources in Literature, Memoirs, Letters, Governmental Documents, Speeches, Charters, Court Decisions and Constitutions.* St. Louis, MO: AmeriSearch, 2001.

Feinberg, J. S., P. D. Feinberg, and A. Huxley. *Ethics for a Brave New World.* Wheaton, Ill.: Crossway Books, 1996.

Freiberg, Kevin and Jackie Freiberg. *Nuts! Southwest Airlines' Crazy Recipe for Business and Personal Success.* Austin, Texas: Bard Press, 1996.

Harris, Sam. *The End of Faith: Religion, Terror and the Future of Reason.* New York: W. W. Norton & Company, 2005.

Huffington, Arianna. *Pigs At The Trough: How Corporate Greed and Political Corruption Are Undermining America.* New York, New York: Three Rivers Press, 2003.

Hutto, Gary W. *Handbook of Mortgage Banking Financial Management.* 2nd ed. Washington, DC: Mortgage Bankers Association, 2005.

_____. *Handbook of Mortgage Lending.* Washington, DC: Mortgage Bankers Association, 2003.

_____. "Preparing for the Future through Scenario Planning

Techniques." *Commercial Mortgage Insight* 4 (July 1999): 10.

James, Jennifer. *Thinking in the Future Tense: Leadership Skills for a New Age.* New York: Simon & Schuster, 1996.

Jamieson, Robert, and A. R. Fausset. *A Commentary, Critical and Explanatory on the Old and New Testaments.* Oak Harbor, WA: Logos Research Systems, Inc., 1997.

Jones, James D. *Strategic Planning for Mortgage Lenders: Positioning Your Company for Success.* Washington, D.C.: Mortgage Bankers Association of America, 1995.

Merriam-Webster's Collegiate Dictionary. 10th.ed. Springfield, Mass.: Merriam-Webster, 1996.

Nave, Orville J. *Nave's Topical Bible: A Digest of the Holy Scriptures.* Peabody, Massachusetts: Hendrickson Publishers, n.d.

New American Standard Bible. 1995 Update. La Habra, California: The Lockman Foundation, 1996.

New Bible Dictionary. Edited by D. R. W. Wood and I. Howard Marshall. 3rd ed. Downers Grove: InterVarsity Press, 1996.

The NIV Study Bible, New International Version. Grand Rapids Michigan: Zondervan Publishing House, 1985.

Nofsinger, John and Kenneth Kim. *Infectious Greed.* Upper Saddle River, NJ: Prentice Hall Financial Times, 2003.

Oxford NIV Scofield Study Bible. Edited by C. I. Scofield. New International Version. New York: Oxford University Press, 1978.

Peters, Thomas J. and Robert H. Waterman, Jr. *In Search of Excellence: Lessons from America's Best-Run Companies.* Warner Books ed. New York, NY: Warner Books, 1984.

Reichheld, Frederick F. and Thomas Teal. *The Loyalty Effect: The Hidden Force Behind Growth, Profits, and Lasting Value.* Boston: Harvard Business School Press, 1996.

Ries, Al. *Focus: The Future of Your Company Depends On*

It. New York: HarperBusiness, 1996.

Rose, Peter S. *Money and Capital Markets: The Financial System in an Increasingly Global Economy*. 4th ed. Homewood, IL: Richard D. Irwin, Inc., 1992.

Schwartz, Peter. *The Art of the Long View: Paths to Strategic Insight for Yourself and Your Company*. New York: Doubleday, 1996.

Senge, Peter M. *The Fifth Discipline: The Art and Practice of the Learning Organization*. New York: Doubleday, 1990.

Thomas, Robert L. *New American Standard Hebrew-Aramaic and Greek Dictionaries*. Updated Edition. Anaheim: Foundation Publications, Inc., 1998.

Thompson, Frank Charles. *The Thompson Chain-Reference Bible: New International Version*. Second Improved Edition. Indianapolis, Indiana: B.B. Kirkbride Bible Co., Inc., 1984.

Toffler, Barbara Ley and Jennifer Reingold. *Final Accounting: Ambition, Greed and the Fall of Arthur Andersen*. New York: Broadway, 2003.

Van der Heijden, Kees. *Scenarios: The Art of Strategic Conversation*. New York: John Wiley & Sons, 1996.

Vine, W. E., Merrill F. Unger, and William White. *Vine's Complete Expository Dictionary of Old and New Testament Words*. Vol. 2. Nashville: T. Nelson, 1996.

Willis Garry. *What Jesus Meant*. New York: Penguin Group, 2006.

The Wycliffe Bible Encyclopedia. Edited by Charles F. Pfeiffer, Howard Frederic Vos and John Rea. Chicago: Moody Press, 1975.

The Zondervan Pictorial Bible Dictionary. Edited by Merrill C. Tenney. Grand Rapids, Michigan: Regency Reference Library, 1967.